Teaching Pyramid Infant–Toddler Observation Scale (TPITOS™) for Infant–Toddler Classrooms Manual, Research Edition

Teaching Pyramid Infant–Toddler Observation Scale (TPITOS™) for Infant–Toddler Classrooms Manual, Research Edition

by

Kathryn M. Bigelow, Ph.D.
University of Kansas
Kansas City

Judith J. Carta, Ph.D.
University of Kansas
Kansas City

Dwight W. Irvin, Ph.D.
University of Kansas
Kansas City

and

Mary Louise Hemmeter, Ph.D.
Vanderbilt University
Nashville, Tennessee

·P A U L·H·
BROOKES
PUBLISHING C<u>O</u>®

Baltimore • London • Sydney

Paul H. Brookes Publishing Co.
Post Office Box 10624
Baltimore, Maryland 21285-0624
USA

www.brookespublishing.com

Typeset by Absolute Service, Inc., Towson, Maryland.
Manufactured in the United States of America by
Versa Press, Inc., East Peoria, Illinois.

Case studies are composites based on the authors' experiences.

Library of Congress Cataloging-in-Publication Data

Names: Bigelow, Kathryn M., author.
Title: Teaching pyramid infant–toddler observation scale (TPITOS™) for infant–toddler classrooms / by Kathryn M. Bigelow, Ph.D.,
    Juniper Gardens Children's Project, University of Kansas, Judith J. Carta, Ph.D., Juniper Gardens Children's Project, University
    of Kansas, Dwight W. Irvin, Ph.D., Juniper Gardens Children's Project, University of Kansas, Mary Louise Hemmeter, Ph.D.,
    Vanderbilt University.
Description: Research edition. | Baltimore, Maryland, USA: Paul H. Brookes Publishing, Co. [2019] | Includes bibliographical
    references and index.
Identifiers: LCCN 2018025203 | ISBN 9781681252421 (pbk.)
Subjects: LCSH: Early childhood education—Evaluation. | Social skills—Study and teaching (Early childhood) | Observation
    (Educational method)
Classification: LCC LB1139.23 .B52 2019 | DDC 372.21—dc23
LC record available at https://lccn.loc.gov/2018025203

British Library Cataloguing in Publication data are available from the British Library.

2022   2021   2020   2019   2018

10   9   8   7   6   5   4   3   2   1

Contents

About the TPITOS Excel Scoring Spreadsheets

The TPITOS Excel Scoring Spreadsheet is a tool for summarizing and graphing TPITOS data. There are four versions of the spreadsheet available: two spreadsheets for PC users and two spreadsheets for Mac users. One file has the capacity to enter data for up to 10 teachers, whereas the other has the capacity to enter data for up to 40 teachers. The four files are

1. TPITOS Excel Scoring Spreadsheet for PC

2. TPITOS Excel Scoring Spreadsheet for PC: 40 Teacher Capacity

3. TPITOS Excel Scoring Spreadsheet for MAC

4. TPITOS Excel Scoring Spreadsheet for MAC: 40 Teacher Capacity

The spreadsheets function in the same way. The TPITOS Excel Scoring Spreadsheet is recommended for use with individual classrooms. The TPITOS Excel Scoring Spreadsheet: 40 Teacher Capacity is more appropriate for larger program evaluation or for planning programwide professional development efforts.

Instructions and a demonstration video are also provided. The four spreadsheets, scoring instructions, and video are available at www.brookespublishing.com/tpitos-scoring-spreadsheet

About the Authors

Kathryn M. Bigelow, Ph.D., is Assistant Research Professor at the Juniper Gardens Children's Project in the Life Span Institute at the University of Kansas. Her research focuses on interventions for culturally and linguistically diverse children and families experiencing multiple risks. Specifically, her work has addressed early childhood language and social-emotional development and the translation of evidence-based interventions for parents, care providers, home visitors, and early intervention providers within both center-based and home-based early childhood education programs. Dr. Bigelow's work in these areas maintains an emphasis on implementation fidelity and how technology can promote engagement and enhance the implementation of evidence-based interventions. She has been the principal investigator (PI) or co-PI on projects focusing on child language promotion and parent engagement in home visiting. Currently, she directs, with Drs. Carta, Irvin, and Hemmeter, an Institute of Education Sciences (IES)–funded research project focused on developing the Infant–Toddler Pyramid Model, a three-tiered model to promote social-emotional outcomes for infants and toddlers, based on the Teaching Pyramid Infant–Toddler Observation Scale (TPITOS™).

Judith J. Carta, Ph.D., is Senior Scientist in the Life Span Institute, Professor of Special Education, and Associate Director of the Juniper Gardens Children's Project at the University of Kansas. Her research focuses on developing strategies to minimize the effects of poverty on children's outcomes and designing practices that teachers and parents can use to promote children's early learning and social-emotional development, methods for monitoring the progress of young children, and strategies for promoting family engagement in early intervention programs. She has been the principal investigator of several multisite research projects and centers funded by the National Institutes of Health, the Institute of Education Sciences (IES), and the Administration on Children and Families. She currently co-directs an IES–funded project to develop the Infant–Toddler Pyramid Model, a three-tiered model to promote social-emotional outcomes for infants and toddlers, based on the Teaching Pyramid Infant–Toddler Observation Scale (TPITOS™). She was a member of the Federal Advisory Panel on Head Start Research and Evaluation and the Division for Early Childhood's Commission on Recommended Practices. Dr. Carta also has served as Editor of *Topics in Early Childhood Special Education* and on the boards of numerous scientific journals. She received the Mary E. McEvoy Service to the Field Award from the Division for Early Childhood.

Dwight W. Irvin, Ph.D., is Assistant Research Professor at the Juniper Gardens Children's Project in the Life Span Institute at the University of Kansas. He was a Response to Intervention in Early Childhood Postdoctoral Fellow at Juniper Gardens Children's Project and a postdoctoral scholar in Department of Education Leadership at the University of Kentucky. His research focuses on the use of wearable sensors to better understand the link between adult–child and child–peer interactions and the social competence of young children at risk for or with identified disabilities in the classroom, home, and community.

Mary Louise Hemmeter, Ph.D., is Professor in the Department of Special Education at Vanderbilt University. Her research focuses on effective instruction, social-emotional development, and challenging behavior and on coaching teachers. She has been a principal investigator (PI) or co-PI on numerous projects funded by the U.S. Departments of Education and Health and Human Services. Through her work on the National Center on the Social Emotional Foundations for Early Learning and Institute of Education Sciences (IES)–funded research projects, she was involved in the development of the *Pyramid Model for Supporting Social Emotional Competence in Young Children* and Practice-Based Coaching, a model for supporting teachers in implementing effective practices. She is currently the PI on an IES–funded development project on programwide supports for implementing the *Pyramid Model*, a co-PI on an IES development project on implementing the Pyramid Model in infant–toddler settings, and a co-PI on an IES efficacy study examining approaches to supporting teachers in implementing embedded instruction. She was a co-editor of the *Journal of Early Intervention* and President of the Council for Exceptional Children's Division for Early Childhood. She received the Mary McEvoy Service to the Field Award from the Division for Early Childhood.

Acknowledgments

The Teaching Pyramid Infant–Toddler Observation Scale (TPITOS™) was initially developed as part of the Technical Assistance Center on Social Emotional Intervention for Young Children (TACSEI). We would like to acknowledge the support of our TACSEI partners: Lise Fox, Phil Strain, Ron Roybal, Barbara Smith, Karen Blasé, Erin Barton, Deb Perry, and Roxanne Kaufman. This early work, as well as the work on the Center on the Social and Emotional Foundations for Early Learning (CSEFEL), resulted in the development of the *Pyramid Model*. This work continues thanks to our Pyramid Model Consortium partners, whose expertise, experience, and commitment to supporting the social-emotional development of young children has been instrumental in supporting our work on the TPITOS: Erin Barton, Ted Bovey, Rob Corso, Glen Dunlap, Lise Fox, Rosa Milagros Santos Gilbertz, Neal Horen, Amy Hunter, Michaelene Ostrosky, Patricia Snyder, Phil Strain, and Tweety Yates.

The TPITOS was developed and refined over the course of many years, and we thank Kathleen Baggett, Amy Hunter, and Phil Strain for their early contributions, which laid the foundation for the current version of the TPITOS. We have had the good fortune to collaborate with Southeast Kansas Community Action Program on development and refinement of the TPITOS, and we thank Linda Broyles, Linda Wilson, Susan Jack, and Joanie Burke for being excellent partners in this work and for providing constructive feedback that shaped the TPITOS into what it is today. In Tennessee, we were fortunate to work with Mid-Cumberland Head Start and the Susan Gray School for Children, and we thank Sone-Serea Batton and Michelle Wyatt for their support of this work. We are also especially appreciative of Myrna Veguilla, who developed the TPITOS Excel Scoring Spreadsheets.

We have been fortunate to have developed long-term collaborative partnerships with infant–toddler professionals throughout the country who have shared their expertise to help refine the TPITOS. We thank the network of infant–toddler professionals who used the TPITOS in their programs and shared their invaluable feedback with us on many occasions. We extend a special thanks to Jessica Hardy, Sarah Heal, Katrina Miller, Alana Schnitz, Kristin Tenney-Blackwell, and Linda Wilson. We also thank Brookes Publishing, Melissa Solarz, and Johanna Schmitter for supporting this work. We have also greatly appreciated the support and assistance of Jenne Accurso Bryant, Sarah Feldmiller, April Fleming, Tara Hixson, Abby Taylor, and Amy Turcotte, as well as Jennifer Amilivia, Stephen Crutchfield, Shu-Fei Tsai, and the teachers and children at Project Eagle Early Head Start.

CHAPTER 1

Introduction to the Teaching Pyramid Infant–Toddler Observation Scale

The *Teaching Pyramid Infant–Toddler Observation Scale (TPITOS™) for Infant–Toddler Classrooms Manual, Research Edition*, is an assessment instrument designed to measure the fidelity of implementation of practices associated with the *Pyramid Model* in center-based infant and toddler care settings. The TPITOS provides a classroom snapshot of the adult behaviors and classroom-environment variables associated with supporting and promoting the social-emotional development of infants and toddlers (birth to 3 years). The *Pyramid Model* is a multi-tiered framework that organizes empirically supported teaching practices for promoting social-emotional competence and addressing challenging behavior (Fox, Dunlap, Hemmeter, Joseph, & Strain, 2003; Hemmeter, Ostrosky, & Fox, 2006).

The development of the *Pyramid Model* was influenced by public health models of promotion, prevention, and intervention practices (Gordon, 1983; Simeonsson, 1991) and schoolwide multi-tiered systems of positive behavior intervention and supports (Horner et al., 2005). The *Pyramid Model* (Fox et al., 2003; Hemmeter et al., 2006) includes universal, secondary, and tertiary teaching practices. Tier 1 (see Figure 1.1) provides *universal promotion* for all children, Tier 2 provides *secondary prevention* to address the intervention needs of children at risk for social-emotional delays, and Tier 3 provides *tertiary interventions* needed for children with persistent challenging behavior.

The first tier of the *Pyramid Model* involves two sets of practices: 1) nurturing and responsive caregiving relationships and 2) high-quality, supportive environments. In this universal tier, *Nurturing and responsive relationships* refers to the relationship between the teacher and the child, the developing partnerships with families, and collaborative relationships among classroom team members and other allied health professionals. *High-quality, supportive environments* refers to the design of safe environments, activities, and schedules that promote active engagement, learning, and appropriate behavior. The TPITOS is a measure of teacher implementation of the universal tier focusing on nurturing and responsive caregiving relationships and high-quality, supportive environments.

THE IMPORTANCE OF SOCIAL-EMOTIONAL DEVELOPMENT

In the United States today, growing numbers of children are attending quality preschool programs (Child Trends Databank, 2014). Attending sound early educational

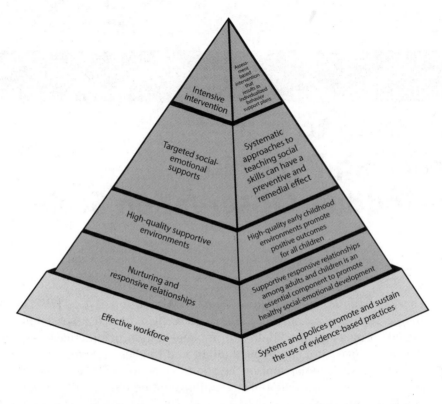

Figure 1.1. The *Pyramid Model.* (From Center on Social and Emotional Foundations for Early Learning at Vanderbilt University. [2003]. *Pyramid Model for promoting social and emotional competence in infants and young children.* Nashville, TN: Author.)

programs greatly enhances children's likelihood of success when they enter primary school (Campbell, Pungello, Miller-Johnson, Burchinal, & Ramey, 2001; National Research Council and Institute of Medicine, 2000). Unfortunately, thousands of preschoolers are suspended or expelled from preschool each year and miss the opportunity to benefit from preschool (U.S. Department of Health and Human Services & U.S. Department of Education, 2015). Furthermore, many young children receive their early care in settings that are sorely lacking in the type of nurturing, responsive interactions known to foster social-emotional development and later self-regulation and executive functioning. It has never been more important to help teachers in early education programs learn how to support young children's social-emotional development. Teachers equipped with the knowledge and skills to provide children with strong social-emotional foundations are much more likely to *prevent* challenging behaviors from occurring and more likely to understand how best to *intervene* when challenging situations occur.

Many early childhood programs adopting the *Pyramid Model* serve infants and toddlers (Fox et al., 2003; Hemmeter et al., 2006). However, there is currently limited information available on how to adapt and align the pyramid approach to meet the needs of children younger than 3 years. We developed the TPITOS to provide a tool that can be used to measure how well practitioners implement the foundation of the *Pyramid Model* with infants and toddlers—the universal practices that teachers and caregivers can use to foster responsive and nurturing relationships with children and provide supportive classroom environments. Data gathered by using the TPITOS are then used to provide feedback to teachers or caregivers, to classroom teams, or to entire programs.

ORGANIZATION OF THE TPITOS

The TPITOS Scoring Form is made up of three types of items: 1) Observational Items, 2) Interview Items, and 3) Red Flags. An *Item* is a category of teacher behavior and represents practices associated with the *Pyramid Model*. Each Item includes two to nine *Indicators* that describe a specific aspect of teacher behavior. Observers score each Indicator based on their observation of the teacher demonstrating the practice during the 2-hour observation or from the teacher's interview responses. The TPITOS also includes Red Flags, which pinpoint specific concerns that may compromise children's social-emotional development. Red Flags are organized into four categories: 1) Responsive to Individual Children, 2) Promoting Emotional Expression and Social Interaction, 3) Responsive to Children's Distress and Challenging Behavior, and 4) Environmental Support for Social Engagement. Observers score Red Flags based on their occurrence during the observation period.

Observational Items

There are 13 Observational Items, or categories of teacher behavior, that represent practices that support and promote social-emotional development. For example, Item 5 states, "Teacher is responsive to children's expression of emotions and teaches about feelings." Observational Items are measured through direct observation. For each Item, there are two to nine Indicators that describe a specific aspect of the teacher's behavior. For example, an Indicator for Item 5 states, "Teacher uses opportunities during activities to teach about feelings." These Indicators are defined in greater detail in the indicator elaborations in Chapter 4.

The Observational Items are scored based on the presence or absence of specific practices carried out by the teacher being observed. This means that the observer gives the teacher a score of *Yes* when the behavior is present, *No* if the behavior does not occur, or *N/A* if the Item or Indicator is not applicable. An observer carrying out a TPITOS observation will follow and record the behavior of one specific teacher on these practices within at least three of four of the following routines for a 2-hour period: free play (e.g., child selects toys from a shelf), structured group activity (e.g., circle time), care routines (e.g., diapering or toileting), and outdoor activities (e.g., sandbox play). Definitions for these routines are included in Chapter 4.

Interview Items

The TPITOS includes an interview that follows the 2-hour observation. Certain items are scored based on the teacher's responses to interview questions. There are also some Indicators that are scored by either observation or interview, as indicated by boxes that show *Obs.* and *Int.* in the Notes column of the TPITOS Scoring Form. For these Items, observers should first try to provide a score based on the classroom observation. If the observation does not provide enough information or evidence to score that Indicator, then the observer can ask the related interview question and use the teacher's response to score that Indicator as *Yes*, *No*, or *N/A*.

Red Flags

During the 2-hour observation, the observer will also record the presence of Red Flags, which are practices that are not consistent with *Pyramid Model* practices and that identify specific concerns that may compromise children's social-emotional development.

Such behaviors may be earmarked as "top priority" for coaching or professional development. An example of a Red Flag is, "Teacher rarely speaks to and/or engages children." The descriptions of the 11 Red Flags are found in Chapter 4. Observers should be familiar with the Red Flags and consider them throughout the observation. Most Red Flags focus on the teacher being observed, though a few are scored for the overall classroom.

ORGANIZATION OF THE TPITOS MANUAL

The TPITOS manual includes background information on the *Pyramid Model for Promoting Social Emotional Competence in Infants and Young Children* and the use of the TPITOS to measure the fidelity with which teachers of infants and toddlers implement the *Pyramid Model* practices. The manual provides users with guidance on how to administer and score the TPITOS and how to interpret TPITOS results. Case studies help make this information come alive by providing real-life examples of the ways in which teacher-specific TPITOS data can be used to coach individual teachers. Case studies also illustrate the approach for using programwide data to guide professional development for an entire program. Finally, the manual includes a section on Frequently Asked Questions.

ADMINISTRATION OF THE TPITOS

An observer carrying out a TPITOS observation will follow and record the behavior of one specific teacher on the practice items within four different routines for a 2-hour period: free play, structured group activity, care routines, and outdoor activities.

When administering the TPITOS, the observer will use a scoring form. The TPITOS Scoring Form includes brief instructions for completing the assessment, followed by the Items and Indicators (Observation, Interview, and Red Flags) that will be scored through observation or interview, a place to note the start and ending time of the observation, a place to make notes about the children and adults present in the classroom during the observation, a chart for tracking the classroom schedule, and each part of the TPITOS to be completed during the observation and interview. Space for making notes during the observation and writing answers during the interview is also provided on the TPITOS Scoring Form. It also includes a Scoring Summary for summarizing the scores for Observational Items, Interview Items, and Red Flags.

Summary scores are obtained for each item by calculating the percentage of indicators present for each item. A TPITOS Excel Scoring Spreadsheet is available for calculating summary scores and graphing TPITOS data at one point in time or across up to three observations for individual teachers, teaching teams, or programs. Additional scoring guidance is included in Chapters 4 and 5.

POTENTIAL USES OF THE TPITOS

One of the fundamental goals of programs for infants and toddlers is promoting children's social-emotional growth and well-being. This goal is incorporated into policy regulations in national programs such as Head Start, as well as organizations providing care to children through early educational centers or child care. TPITOS data may be used to support professional development for early educators or child care practitioners in the following ways: 1) identifying and making explicit the specific competencies that promote social-emotional development, 2) providing team and individual teacher feedback to reinforce teacher strengths, 3) guiding individual and team targeted goal-setting to strengthen teacher competencies, and 4) monitoring growth relevant to teacher competencies or quality-improvement initiatives.

The TPITOS can also be used in research studies to measure implementation fidelity and change over time. The TPITOS may be used, for example, to describe the fidelity of implementation of the first tier (universal practices) of the *Pyramid Model* when implemented in a specific classroom, a group of classrooms, or a group of programs. The TPITOS can also be used to measure whether teachers' implementation of specific practices changes after an intervention focused on changing teacher behaviors.

RESEARCH BACKGROUND OF THE TPITOS

The first few years of a child's life are a critical time. In years 1–3, children develop a foundation for healthy social-emotional development or, alternately, begin a trajectory for social and academic delays and disabilities (National Research Council & Institute of Medicine, 2000). Approximately 10%–15% of children between birth and 5 years of age experience social-emotional difficulties that negatively affect their functioning and school readiness (Brauner & Stephens, 2006; Brown, Copeland, Sucharew, & Kahn, 2012). Of particular concern are children from low-income neighborhoods with multiple risk factors—these children are much more likely to experience behavioral problems early in life (Cooper, Masi, & Vick, 2009; Duncan, Brooks-Gunn & Klebanov, 1994). In addition, children whose families experience environmental risks, such as domestic violence exposure, substance use, and mental health issues, are more likely to experience social-emotional difficulties (Cabaj, McDonald, & Tough, 2014). Especially noteworthy is the fact that interventions focused on children's early caregiving interactions can typically alleviate or reverse about 50% of the adverse effects of poverty on children's social-emotional development (Duncan & Brooks-Gunn, 2000).

There are no existing studies that have tested the effectiveness of an entire tiered model to prevent challenging behavior and promote the social-emotional development of infants and toddlers. However, considerable research exists on the effectiveness of the *components* of such a model, such as scaffolding, establishing routines, and supporting infants' peer interactions (Copple & Bredekamp, 2009; Landry, Smith, Swank, & Guttentag, 2008). Many of these specific practices have been highlighted as Recommended Practices by the Division of Early Childhood (DEC; Division for Early Childhood, 2014). One category of the DEC Recommended Practices focuses specifically on interactional practices between the caregiver and child, such as "observing, interpreting, and responding contingently" to children's emotional expressions or encouraging children, "to initiate or sustain positive interactions with other children and adults during routines and activities through modeling, teaching, and feedback" (p. 27). These practices have been identified in the literature as essential for promoting infant–toddler social-emotional and communication development (Guttentag et al., 2014; Landry et al., 2008). Another category of DEC Recommended Practices addresses specific instructional practices measured by the TPITOS, such as, "embedding instruction within and across routines, activities, and environments to provide contextually relevant learning opportunities" (p. 11) and, "using explicit feedback and consequences to increase child engagement, play, and skills" (p. 11). The TPITOS focuses on these critical elements for supporting and guiding children's social-emotional growth and distills them into observable teacher behaviors.

In the next chapter, we provide more information about the development of TPITOS and key practices assessed using TPITOS, including descriptions of TPITOS Items and Indicators.

CHAPTER 2

Overview of the *Pyramid Model* and the Teaching Pyramid Infant–Toddler Observation Scale

Public health models, which provided a tiered framework of promotion, prevention, and intervention, informed early *Pyramid Model* development (Gordon, 1983; Simeonsson, 1991). These frameworks typically incorporate *universal promotion strategies*, which address the needs of all members of a population; *secondary strategies* for those who are at risk for adverse outcomes as a means of prevention; and *tertiary strategies* for those who have already experienced negative outcomes or require more intensive interventions. This three-tiered approach has been applied to the prevention and intervention of challenging behavior in K–12 schools in the form of Positive Behavior Support (Horner et al., 2005) and has been effective in reducing challenging behavior and increasing academic learning time. The *Pyramid Model* applies this three-tiered approach to the social-emotional development needs of young children, some of whom are at risk for or have developed challenging behavior (Fox, Dunlap, Hemmeter, Joseph, & Strain, 2003; Hemmeter, Ostrosky, & Fox, 2006).

The *Pyramid Model* was developed through the work of two federally funded research and training centers, the Center on the Social and Emotional Foundations for Early Learning (CSEFEL) and the Technical Assistance Center on Social Emotional Intervention for Young Children (TACSEI). The model is a promotion, prevention, and intervention framework to organize and guide decision making about the implementation of practices that have been demonstrated to support social-emotional development and prevent challenging behavior in young children (Fox et al., 2003; Hemmeter et al., 2006). Extensive research on the model and its associated practices have supported its use within early child care and educational systems (Hemmeter, Snyder, Fox, & Algina, 2011, 2016). Teachers who have been given systematic professional development (PD) in the model with specific practice-based coaching have sustained their use of the pyramid practices a year after the PD intervention (Hemmeter, Fox, Snyder, & Algina, 2016, April). The model is currently being implemented state-wide in 28 states and territories, and *Pyramid Model* trainings have been provided in all 50 states and territories over the last decade. To date, the *Pyramid Model* has reached more than 250,000 early childhood providers nationally and 43 countries internationally. *Pyramid Model* trainings and technical assistance are available and address implementation of the *Pyramid Model* at the teacher, program, and state levels.

The Teaching Pyramid Observation Tool (TPOT™) has been an important resource for ensuring that the *Pyramid Model* is implemented with high quality in preschool settings (Fox, Hemmeter, & Snyder, 2014). The TPOT is an assessment designed to measure teachers' implementation of the *Pyramid Model* and its specific teaching and behavior supports for early childhood classrooms serving children 2–5 years of age. This tool has been used to provide feedback to teachers and programs on how those specific practices have been implemented in preschool settings. The Teaching Pyramid Infant–Toddler Observation Scale (TPITOS™) was developed to provide this type of information about implementation of *Pyramid Model* practices in programs serving infants and toddlers.

DEVELOPMENT OF THE TPITOS

Unlike the TPOT, the TPITOS has been developed to measure only the first, or universal, tier of the *Pyramid Model* (i.e., the nurturing and responsive caregiving relationships and high-quality, supportive environments). Earlier versions of the TPITOS differed in the format of the Observational Items and structure of the tool. The TPITOS has undergone significant field testing and revision through ongoing collaboration with an extensive national network of professionals who support infant and toddler programs as coaches, supervisors, program administrators, and researchers. The scope of the items has been refined over the years to reflect the priorities and recommended practices for infant and toddler care (e.g., Division of Early Childhood Recommended Practices) and align with resources such as the Infant–Toddler Modules developed by CSEFEL. The Infant–Toddler Modules provide training on how to implement the practices associated with the *Pyramid Model* and include presentation handouts, videos, and activities aimed at supporting high-quality implementation of the *Pyramid Model* in infant and toddler settings.

PRACTICES ASSESSED BY THE TPITOS

The TPITOS measures 13 Items that represent practices related to teacher behavior. Each Item is made up of a set of *Indicators* that are scored based on observation or interview. For each of the 13 Items, there are two to nine Indicators that represent a specific teaching practice. Observers score each Indicator with a *Yes* or a *No* based on their observation of the teacher demonstrating the practice during the 2-hour observation or the teacher's interview responses. The TPITOS also includes 11 Red Flags, which are practices that are inconsistent with the *Pyramid Model* and require immediate attention because they are counterproductive to the implementation of practices that promote social and emotional competence in young children. Identifying the presence of Red Flags can help pinpoint specific concerns that may compromise children's social-emotional development. Red Flags are organized into four categories: Responsive to Individual Children, Promoting Emotional Expression and Social Interaction, Responsive to Children's Distress and Challenging Behavior, and Environmental Support for Social Engagement.

Instructions on preparing for and structuring the observation can be found in Chapter 3. Instructions for scoring each Item and the associated Indicators, as well as the Red Flags, are included in Chapter 4.

TPITOS Items and Indicators

TPITOS practices and their Indicators are described here:

1. **Teacher provides opportunities for communication and building relationships.** The amount and quality of language provided to infants and toddlers is crucial for their development and is an important element of responsive and engaging interactions. This Item focuses on teachers' talk to children, the manner in which teachers talk to children, and the types of talk in which a teacher engages. This includes commenting on children's interests, listening and responding to encourage child communication, providing opportunities for social interactions, and providing alternative strategies for communicating with children who are nonverbal, have language delays, or are dual language learners (DLLs).

2. **Teacher demonstrates warmth and responsivity to individual children.** Sensitive and responsive interactions are the foundation for promoting a child's social-emotional competence. This item focuses on the strategies teachers use to demonstrate warmth and responsivity toward all children in the classroom, such as warm and responsive tone, eye contact, physical affection, body position at a child's level, warm greetings, and engagement in play.

3. **Teacher promotes positive peer interactions.** Challenging behavior can result when children do not have the skills necessary to interact in positive ways with their peers. This Item focuses on the practices teachers use to teach and support children during peer interactions. Practices addressed include encouraging children to be aware of and care about their peers and their intentions, helping children initiate and maintain interactions, supporting peer interactions through positive comments, and providing support when negative interactions occur.

4. **Teacher promotes children's active engagement.** Children's active engagement in activities and routines is critical for their development and for preventing challenging behavior. This Item focuses on the manner in which teachers encourage and support child engagement across routines, such as encouraging unengaged children to become engaged, using a variety of strategies to support engagement, supporting sustained engagement, and providing opportunities for toddlers to make choices.

5. **Teacher is responsive to children's expression of emotions and teaches about feelings.** Children experience a variety of emotions, and teachers are crucial in helping children learn what these emotions represent and how to manage emotions such as happiness, sadness, frustration, anger, and excitement. This Item focuses on practices, such as helping children name and describe their emotions, using naturally occurring opportunities to teach about feelings, and individualizing these practices based on children's developmental needs. This item also addresses how teachers label and regulate their own emotions in the classroom.

6. **Teacher communicates and provides feedback about developmentally appropriate behavioral expectations.** Establishing developmentally appropriate behavioral expectations is a proactive way to teach children what is expected and prevent challenging behavior, as opposed to simply responding to

instances of challenging behavior when they occur. This can also lay the foundation for redirection when it is necessary for teachers to respond to challenging behavior. Practices include establishing expectations that are developmentally appropriate to the children in the classroom, communicating and demonstrating these expectations verbally and through modeling, acknowledging appropriate behavior when it occurs, using simple words to explain the natural consequences of undesirable behavior, and anticipating potential conflict situations before they occur.

7. **Teacher responds to children in distress and manages challenging behaviors.** Instances of challenging behavior can occur in infant and toddler classrooms, but in many cases, these behaviors are considered common occurrences among this age group. Behaviors such as biting, taking toys from other children, or crying and throwing tantrums can be challenging behaviors but are not unexpected or uncommon in infant and toddler settings. Thus, these challenging behaviors may be viewed as "challenging situations" to teachers versus challenging behaviors. Practices observed include teachers maintaining a calm, supportive, and positive tone during distressful or challenging episodes; responding to and supporting children in distress; providing positive attention once the episode has ended; using challenging situations as an opportunity to recognize and deal with emotions; and using strategies such as redirection or planned ignoring.

8. **Teacher uses specific strategies or modifications for children with disabilities/delays or who are DLLs.** To determine whether children who have disabilities or delays or who are DLLs are present within the classroom, observers inquire with the teacher about this before the observation and record this information on the cover page. Practices addressed by this Item include modifications or supports that teachers use to support social-emotional development with children who have disabilities or delays or who are DLLs.

9. **Teacher conveys predictability through a carefully planned schedule, routines, and transitions.** Having a consistent and predictable schedule of routines and structuring transitions to engage and support children can reduce instances of challenging behavior and support learning. Practices include having a schedule posted for the general routines throughout the day, following that schedule, but varying it to accommodate the needs of individual children. This also includes using verbal and visual cues and predictable routines to support children in transitions in developmentally and individually appropriate ways.

10. **Environment is arranged to foster social-emotional development.** The physical layout of a classroom environment can impact the way children explore and how teachers and children interact. Practices addressed by this Item include the presence of a variety of toys and play areas to support engagement and social interaction, ample materials for the children present, and the availability of books and other materials to promote social awareness.

11. **Teacher collaborates with his or her peers (e.g., other teachers, mental health practitioners, allied health professionals) to support children's social-emotional development.** The base of the *Pyramid Model* involves an effective workforce. One element of that is a teaching team that works well together, communicates, and ensures that the needs of all children in the classroom

are met throughout the day. This Item addresses the manner in which teachers collaborate in a classroom to engage children in a positive manner, follow the classroom schedule of routines, and share information with allied professionals who are working with children in the classroom.

12. **Teacher has effective strategies for engaging parents in supporting their children's social-emotional development and addressing challenging behaviors.** Families are crucial in promoting their children's social-emotional development. Many of the practices that teachers use in the classroom are applicable at home and should be communicated to families in supportive ways. This helps families adapt and use those strategies meaningfully at home and in the community. Families should also be involved when there are instances of challenging behavior or distress or other social-emotional concerns. This Item addresses the manner in which teachers engage parents in supporting social-emotional development. Practices that are rated include the way in which teachers share information and strategies related to social-emotional development and challenging behavior with families and how teachers work together with families when there are concerns.

13. **Teacher has effective strategies for communicating with families and promoting family involvement in the classroom.** Strong partnerships between parents and teachers are instrumental, and family engagement in the classroom is an important element. It is important that teachers communicate with families in ways that keep the lines of communication open with each family and ensure parents and teachers have the information they need. This Item addresses the manner in which teachers share information about the classroom with families, how they communicate about daily experiences, how teachers obtain information from families about how children are doing at home, and how teachers promote parent engagement in the classroom.

Red Flags

There are 11 Red Flags that describe teacher behaviors that may compromise children's social-emotional development. Red Flags are scored either for the teacher being observed or for the classroom. These Items address teacher responsivity, emotional expression, social interaction, and teacher response to children's distress and challenging behavior. Note that examples and nonexamples of Red Flag behaviors are included in Chapter 4.

1. Children spend large amounts of time disengaged, without assistance from this teacher to become engaged.

2. Teacher rarely speaks to and/or engages children.

3. Teacher seldom makes eye contact with children during interactions.

4. Classroom staff expect children in the class to be on the same schedule for activities such as feeding or diapering instead of attending to individual children's needs for personal care.

5. Teacher uses flat affect when talking with infants and toddlers.

6. Teacher speaks harshly to children.

7. Children seem generally unhappy or upset.

8. Children who are distressed are left unattended.

9. When problem behaviors occur, teacher uses punitive practices.

10. The environment is set up such that children are isolated from each other for long periods of time.

11. The environment is arranged in a way that prevents children from engaging with materials, toys, and/or activities.

SUMMARY

In this chapter, we provided background information about the *Pyramid Model*, described the procedures used to develop the TPITOS, and provided an overview of the practices assessed by the TPITOS. The next chapter describes how to administer the TPITOS, including procedures for conducting an observation and the interview.

CHAPTER 3

Using the Teaching Pyramid Infant–Toddler Observation Scale

The procedures for administering the TPITOS are described in this chapter, including how to prepare for, conduct, and conclude the TPITOS observation and interview. Training is strongly recommended prior to using the TPITOS.

Prior to conducting a TPITOS observation, it is helpful to be familiar with the classroom and its daily schedule. It is also important to prepare and be familiar with the materials needed for an observation. Have the manual with Indicator Elaborations on hand, as well as the TPITOS Scoring Form and a note pad for taking notes. It is recommended that observers plan to take detailed notes throughout the observation, so it will be helpful to have a place within the classroom to sit and a clipboard or other writing surface on which to take notes. It is also important for observers to be able to change positions or move around the room to observe and hear the teacher. Finally, observations should be conducted on days when the teacher will be present for a 2-hour period and when the typical schedule is followed (e.g., no field trips or special guests).

PREPARING FOR THE OBSERVATION

To complete the TPITOS, the observer should structure the observation to observe *one teacher at a time* for *at least a 2-hour period* and then allow an additional 20 minutes after the observation to conduct the teacher interview. We recommend that the teacher be observed across at least *three different types of routines*, for a minimum of 15 minutes per routine within that 2-hour observation period. The categories of routines include free play, structured group, personal care, and outdoor activities. For any given classroom, this may require multiple observations in order to observe each teacher in that classroom (e.g., two observations to observe two teachers). The TPITOS was designed to be used to observe one teacher at a time rather than observing two teachers concurrently, so that TPITOS data and observation notes can be used to provide individualized feedback. If you observe notable practices used by a teacher you are not actively observing (e.g., a Red Flag), you may make a brief note on the TPITOS Scoring Form. It is not recommended, however, that observers attempt to complete the TPITOS for more than one teacher at the same time to avoid missing important yet brief interactions.

It is also recommended that the 2-hour observation for one teacher be conducted in one observational session (i.e., 2 continuous hours on 1 day). In instances in which teachers leave the classroom before the end of the 2-hour observation period

13

(e.g., attending a meeting outside of the classroom after 1 hour), observations can be conducted over 2 days without more than a few days between each observation. It is important not to break the observation up over more than 2 days or observe in segments that are shorter than 1 hour.

Observations should be structured so the teachers and children present, and the routines observed are representative of the conditions that are typical for that setting. In a center-based program, general guidelines are that *at least three children* should be present and *at least three different routines* should be observed during the observation. It is important for the observation to capture conditions typical for that setting. Having some familiarity with the classroom may help observers better understand what is typical for that setting.

Before Starting the Observation

Upon arrival, the observer should become oriented to the classroom and the observation period. Ask the teacher what activities will occur during your observation and when they will occur. Confirm that the teacher being observed plans to remain in the classroom for the duration of the observation. Explain that you are interested in observing typical routines and interactions during this 2-hour observation. To prepare to complete the interview Items, ask the teacher if you may spend about 20 minutes talking with him or her after the observation. If this is not feasible immediately after the observation, determine when this might be more convenient for the teacher. The interview could take place within the classroom (i.e., while the teacher is playing on the floor with infants or during a time when most children are napping). The interview may be conducted the next day if necessary, but do not allow too much time to pass, because you need to reflect on the practices and activities observed in the classroom as part of the interview.

Before starting the observation, complete the cover sheet to indicate the following: 1) date of observation, 2) program/center, 3) classroom, 4) teacher name or identification code (ID), 5) observer name or ID, 6) start time of the observation, 7) number of adults present when observation begins, 8) number of children present when observation begins, and 9) age range of the children present (see Figure 3.1). Also, ask if there are children in the classroom present today who are unable to communicate with you in the same way as other children in the class due to language delay, and if there are children who are DLLs. Record the activities or routines observed, their start and end times, total length of time observed in each routine, and any notes regarding those activities on the Schedule of Activities sheet as you conduct the observation. Note when you stopped an observation because of the teacher or children leaving the room or when the observation is suspended (e.g., guests entering the room). You are also prompted to ask the teacher whether there is information that he or she would like to share with you, such as goals for the classroom or recent challenges experienced. Include any notes related to such events on the cover sheet.

Classroom Routines

TPITOS observations are structured so that teacher practices are scored across the different routines that are typical for infant and toddler classrooms. We often see that some teachers implement TPITOS practices with greater fidelity or more frequently in some routines more than others. For instance, some teachers may be highly involved or interactive during structured group activities but less involved during free play

Teaching Pyramid Infant–Toddler Observation Scale (TPITOS™) for Infant–Toddler Classrooms RESEARCH EDITION ▲TPITOS.

Date of observation: *May 11, 2018*   Start time: *8:30 am*

Program/Center name: *Sunshine Center*   End time: *10:40 am*

Classroom name: *Seedlings*

Teacher name/ID: *Rosa*   Observer name/ID: *Sara*

Please note if the observation is interrupted or stopped because the teacher or majority of children leave the classroom or are engaged in an activity or routine that is not observed. If that occurs, indicate the time you stopped the observation, the time the observation was resumed, and the length of time the observation was suspended.

Time observation stopped: *9:15*   Time observation resumed: *9:25*

Length of time (in minutes) the observation was suspended: *10 min*

Notes, *if applicable:* *Three infants will transition to toddler room in June.*

Number of adults present when

observation begins *2*   observation ends *2*

Number of children present when

observation begins *5*   observation ends *6*

Age range of children present:

Years/Months *2 months*   to Years/Months *12 months*

To most effectively answer Item 1 (CBR8) and Item 8, ask the teacher the following questions and record the response PRIOR TO THE OBSERVATION:

"Are there children present today who are unable to communicate with you in the same way as other children in the class because they have language delays or disabilities? If yes, how many?"   ☑ Yes (# of children *2*)   ☐ No

"Are there children present today who need information presented to them in a different way because they are DLLs? If yes, how many?"   ☐ Yes (# of children ____)   ☑ No

OPTIONAL: "Is there additional information you would like to share with me before we begin the observation (e.g., goals, challenges)?" _____

NOTES:

Just completed training on a new curriculum; Interested in working on transitions

Figure 3.1.   Sample cover sheet of the TPITOS Scoring Form.

or outdoor activities. For this reason, it is recommended that a TPITOS observation include at least three different routines. Most classroom activities should fall into one of four types of routines: 1) free play, 2) structured group activities, 3) personal care activities, and 4) outdoor activities (see Table 3.1). Free play is generally characterized by free choice of play activities available or offered to children. Structured group activities include an element of structure or focus, which is typically organized by the teacher. Structured group activities may involve the whole classroom but would typically involve a small group of children and have some degree of organization, such as arts, crafts, or circle time. Diapering, washing hands, feedings, and meals are personal care routines. Outdoor activities are activities that take place outdoors, in a gym, or in larger multi-use room space. It is not necessary to observe all four routines, but it is important to observe teacher behavior across multiple routines.

After 2 hours of observation, if you have observed only two and not three routines, you should decide whether the two routines you have observed have provided you with enough information to accurately reflect that teacher's practice. It is up to the observer to determine whether the observation was truly representative of typical

Table 3.1. Categories of daily routines observed during an observation

Routine	Examples
Free play	Children have free choice of toys
	Children read books independently
	Child chooses to color independently
	Infant explores toys on the floor
	Teacher places a bin of toys out for children to choose from, but without structure or focus
Structured group activities	Finger painting with a small group
	Circle time with a group
	Story time with a small group
	Crafts with a small group or the whole class
	Group singing with musical instruments
Personal care routines	Diapering
	Hand washing
	Lunch
	Bottle feeding
Outdoor activities	Playground play
	Play in the gym

care and interactions in that specific setting or whether additional observation time is needed to observe that teacher engaged in additional routines. This requires that the observer have a level of familiarity with the classroom. If you are not familiar enough with the classroom to know whether the observed practices are typical for that teacher, it is recommended that the length of the observation be extended to observe a third routine. If additional observation time is needed, arrange to stay longer to observe a third routine or return within a few days.

It is understood that the distinction between some activities may be difficult to discern. It may be difficult to decide whether a particular play activity is truly "free play" or a "structured group activity." The purpose for organizing observations into routines is to better inform coaching and professional development. Therefore, observers should use their best judgment in determining the appropriate routine category when there are questions about the type of routine.

CONDUCTING THE OBSERVATION

A TPITOS administration consists of three main elements:

1. Observe a teacher engaged in typical daily classroom routines (free play, structured group, personal care [meals, feeding, diapering], and outdoor activities) while taking detailed notes in order to score each Indicator as *Yes*, *No*, or *N/A*. Indicator Elaborations provide definitions for each practice and guidance on whether the teacher's practice meets the scoring criteria. Elaborations can be found in Chapter 4.

2. Ask interview questions to help you score Items you were unable to score during the classroom observation. Plan to ask interview questions after the observational period. The interview Items expand on many of these observational Items or

pertain to practices that may not be readily observable in a 2-hour period, such as the strategies used to communicate with families.

3. Observe for Red Flags, which are Items that require a *Yes* or *No* response based on observation of either individual teachers or the classroom environment. These are scored during the observation, and scoring is completed after the observation is complete.

Observational Items

Observational Items are organized into 13 Items or categories of teacher behavior. Appendix A lists the two- or three-letter code associated with each Item and the Item name. There are two to nine Indicators under each Item that describe a specific aspect of teacher behavior and are scored as either *Yes* or *No*. These Indicators are defined in greater detail in the Elaborations in Chapter 4.

For Items 1–7, teacher behaviors are scored within individual routines. For each Indicator, a score is given for each routine observed. These Items have columns in which you can record a *Yes* or *No* score for each routine you observe. The score given to the majority of routines within a given Indicator determines the overall Indicator score (e.g., scored *Yes* to two of three observed routines or to three of four observed routines).

For Items 8–13, one score is given for the whole observation. Observers should mark *Yes* or *No* for each Indicator. Some Indicators are scored by either observation or interview, as indicated by boxes that show *Obs.* and *Int.* in the Notes column. Observers should first try to score these Items based on the classroom observation. Then, if the observation does not provide enough information or evidence to score that Indicator, you may then ask the related interview question and use the teacher's response to score that Indicator. Figure 3.2 shows an example of Indicator CAE5, which can be scored based on observation or interview.

Observers indicate *Yes* if the practice was observed or *No* if the practice was not observed, based on criteria provided in the Elaborations for Indicators. Each Elaboration includes scoring criteria and examples for scoring *Yes* and for scoring *No*. Elaborations also indicate whether scoring *Not Applicable (N/A)* is an option. The Indicators for which *N/A* can be scored are identified with a `N/A` on the TPITOS Scoring Form. Write *N/A* in the appropriate row and column for the Indicator and Routine being scored *N/A*. As an example, *N/A* is a possible score for Indicators related to child distress or challenging behavior because an observation might not always include instances of child distress or challenging behavior. In those situations, one could not rate Indicators describing how a teacher responded in those situations, so *N/A* would be the appropriate rating. See Figure 3.3 for an example of an indicator that can be scored *N/A*.

Some Indicators, such as those related to teacher warmth and responsivity, cannot be scored with the *N/A* option because there would never be an observation period in which warmth and responsivity should NOT be scored. In short, if an Elaboration does not include criteria for scoring an Item *N/A*, then it should not be scored with an *N/A*. Appendix B lists all of the Indicators that have the potential to be scored as *N/A*.

Because the TPITOS can be conducted in classrooms serving a large range of ages (i.e., young infants up to 3-year-olds), some Items and Indicators are not relevant for all care settings. For instance, Items addressing challenging behavior or

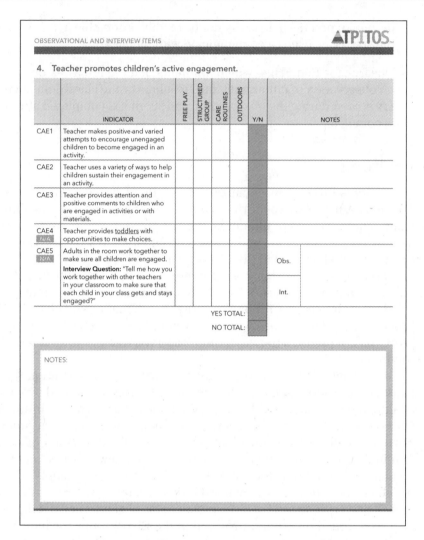

Figure 3.2.   A sample Item with Indicators that can be scored by observation or interview.

peer interactions are more relevant for toddlers than infants. For Items or Indicators that apply to toddler care but not to infant care settings, we have specifically used the word <u>toddlers</u> and underlined it to communicate that these Indicators are specific to *toddlers*. These Items may be scored as *N/A* if they are not applicable to the age group you are observing. For example, in Item 7, "Teacher responds to children in distress and manages challenging behaviors," Indicators RDC1, RDC2, RDC4, and RDC7 apply to both infants and toddlers. However, because Indicators RDC3, RDC5, and RDC6 pertain to practices that would not necessarily be recommended for infants (e.g., providing positive attention for calming down and behaving appropriately, supporting upset toddlers with problem-solving strategies, and using strategies such as redirection and planned ignoring), they would be scored *N/A* when observing in settings that include only infants. See Figure 3.4 for an example of an Item with Indicators that would be scored only for toddlers. Appendix B includes a list of all of the Indicators that are appropriate for toddlers only, as indicated by the word <u>toddler</u> underlined within the Indicator title, and would not be scored in a classroom where there are no toddlers present.

OBSERVATIONAL AND INTERVIEW ITEMS

TPITOS

6. Teacher communicates and provides feedback about developmentally appropriate behavioral expectations.

	INDICATOR	FREE PLAY	STRUCTURED GROUP	CARE ROUTINES	OUTDOORS	Y/N	NOTES
CBE1	Teacher expectations are developmentally appropriate and individualized as needed.						
CBE2 N/A	Teacher communicates behavioral expectations by letting toddlers know, in a positive tone, what they should do in specific activities (and not just what they shouldn't do).						
CBE3	Teacher demonstrates behavioral expectations in specific activities through modeling.						
CBE4	Teacher frequently acknowledges, praises, and/or encourages appropriate behavior related to expectations.						
CBE5 N/A	Teacher uses simple words or phrases to explain natural consequences of engaging in unsafe behavior.						
CBE6 N/A	Teacher provides feedback to toddlers in instances of behavior that does not meet classroom expectations.						
CBE7	Teacher anticipates potential conflict situations or instances in which behavior may not meet classroom expectations and provides guidance to children before the situations get out of control.						Obs.
	Interview Question: "What steps do you take to minimize conflicts between children or prevent behavior that does not meet classroom expectations?"						Int.
					YES TOTAL:		
					NO TOTAL:		

NOTES:

Figure 3.3. Example of an Item with Indicators that can be scored *N/A*.

In some cases, the Elaborations describe criteria that stipulate that some practices should be observed a specified number of times in order to be scored *Yes*. For instance, Item 1, Indicator PPI3, which focuses on practices for helping children initiate positive peer interactions, states that you should score *No* if you see fewer than two instances of that practice. Appendix C includes a compilation of the Items for which a specified frequency is required in the scoring criteria.

During the observation period, it is recommended that observers take extensive notes on the practices teachers use within each routine. Then, after the observation and interview, observers should use their notes to complete the TPITOS Scoring Form. There are multiple strategies for taking notes during the observation. You can create a running log of what teachers say and do and underline or circle key words that will highlight practices. For example, one note might say, "Child getting frustrated about a toy; teacher asked, 'Are you feeling frustrated?'" with the word *frustrated* circled to indicate that the statement the teacher made is proof that he or she asked a question about emotions. Another note-taking strategy involves drawing a line down the page to create a small column on the right side of the page. Then, write your notes

OBSERVATIONAL AND INTERVIEW ITEMS   **△TPITOS**

7. Teacher responds to children in distress and manages challenging behaviors.

	INDICATOR	FREE PLAY	STRUCTURED GROUP	CARE ROUTINES	OUTDOORS	Y/N	NOTES
RDC1 N/A	Teacher's tone remains calm, supportive, and positive during children's distressful or challenging episodes.						
RDC2 N/A	Teacher immediately responds to children in distress to assess children's status.						
RDC3 N/A	Teacher provides positive attention to toddlers when they have calmed down and are behaving appropriately.						
RDC4 N/A	Teacher uses a challenging situation as an opportunity to help children recognize and deal with emotions.						
RDC5 N/A	Teacher provides support to toddlers who are angry or upset to help them with problem solving, when appropriate.						
RDC6 N/A	Teacher uses strategies such as redirection and/or planned ignoring with individual toddlers who are in distress or engage in occasional episodes of challenging behavior.						Obs.
	Interview Question: "Tell me what strategies you follow when children have occasional episodes of challenging behavior (e.g., physical aggression, screaming, taking others' toys)?"						Int.
RDC7 N/A	Teacher uses a variety of strategies to console, soothe, or calm children who are in distress and individualizes responses according to children and situations.						Obs.
	Interview Question: "Tell me about different ways that you comfort children who are in distress (e.g., picking up an infant, problem solving with a toddler)?"						Int.
				YES TOTAL:			
				NO TOTAL:			

NOTES:

Figure 3.4. Example of an Item with Indicators that would be scored only when toddlers are present.

transcribing the activities of the observation on the left and write in key words or abbreviations (e.g., "emotions," "expectations") to cue you to the Items and Indicators represented in the notes in the left column. After note taking during the observation, use your notes to help determine which questions you will ask in the interview.

Interview Items

Interview questions are included to collect information about practices that are not observed during the classroom observation. Indicators for which an interview question is permitted are indicated by *Int.* in the notes column of the TPITOS Scoring Form. In some cases, interview questions are used to score Items that did not happen to occur during the observation (e.g., there were no instances of challenging child behavior), whereas others are used to score Items that are unlikely to be observed during a classroom observation (e.g., how teachers and allied professionals collaborate). A brief interview with the observed teacher should be conducted as soon after the observation period as possible but at a time that is convenient for the teacher.

Be sure to inform the teacher prior to the day of observation that you would like to speak with him or her for about 20 minutes and determine a convenient time.

The interview worksheet at the end of the TPITOS Scoring Form consolidates all of the Items that could be included in the interview. Use this worksheet to guide your interview. You only need to ask the interview questions associated with Indicators you could not score based on the observation. For example, Indicator CAE5 pertains to adults in the room working together to make sure all children are engaged. If during the observation, the observed teacher was the only teacher in the room for most of the observation, and you did not have the opportunity to observe multiple teachers working together to make sure all children were engaged, you would ask this question during the interview using the interview question provided. You would then use the teacher's response to score that Item.

After the observation, go through the TPITOS Scoring Form and review the Indicators for which an interview question is permitted. If you were unable to score an Indicator from the observation, circle *Int.* in the Notes column on the TPITOS Scoring Form. Then, transfer these over to the Interview Worksheet by circling *Int.* in the Notes column. These are the Indicators that should be included in the teacher interview. Wording for the interview questions is provided on the Interview Worksheet. You will be looking for specific examples of the practices and using the criteria in the Indicator Elaborations to determine whether to score *Yes* or *No*. If necessary, ask additional clarifying questions or encourage teachers to elaborate if more information is needed. For instance, the interview question states, "Tell me how you work together with other teachers in your classroom to make sure that each child in your class gets and stays engaged." If additional clarification is needed or if the teacher's response needs clarification, you may ask additional questions, such as, "Can you give me an example of how you and your teaching partner work to involve all of the children in the room in activities throughout the day?" See Figure 3.5 for an example of the Interview Worksheet.

As you ask questions, record teacher responses on the Interview Worksheet. Take detailed notes, because these will inform your scores. After the interview, transfer scores from the Interview Worksheet to the appropriate TPITOS Indicator so that accurate Item totals can be calculated.

After the interview, use teacher responses as well as your notes to score the Indicators. For each Indicator, determine whether the teacher's response would lead you to score the Indicator *Yes* or *No*. To score *Yes*, the teacher's response must indicate the practice is used according to the criteria in the Elaboration. Score *No* if the response does not describe specific strategies or modifications.

To incorporate interview responses into Indicator scoring, follow these guidelines:

1. Ask interview questions only when you cannot give a score of *Yes* or *No* based on the observation. If the teacher engaged in the practice, score *Yes*. If there were opportunities to engage in the practice, and the teacher did not engage in the practice according to the criteria in the Elaboration, score *No*. In both of these cases, do not ask the interview question. The Indicator can be scored based on your observation.

2. Ask interview questions when the opportunities to engage in the practice did not arise or you do not have enough evidence to give a score of *Yes* or *No*. For instance, ask the interview question under Item 7, Indicator RDC6 when you do not have the opportunity to observe redirection or planned ignoring because either there were no challenging child behaviors or those were not the appropriate strategies for the behaviors that did occur. Also ask the interview questions for Indicators

Figure 3.5. A sample interview worksheet.

that are unlikely to be identifiable or seen during the observation, such as Item 11, Indicators TCP5 and TCP6. These Indicators focus on the practices teachers use to communicate with allied professionals and incorporate that information into practice. Then, based on the teacher's responses to the interview questions, determine whether the practices described would lead you to score *Yes*, *No*, or *N/A*.

Red Flags

There are 11 Red Flags, which pinpoint specific concerns that may compromise children's social-emotional development. Red Flags are scored based on whether you see them during the observation period. These Items are organized into four categories: Responsive to Individual Children, Promoting Emotional Expression and Social Interaction, Responds to Children's Distress and Challenging Behavior, and Environmental Support for Social Engagement. See Figure 3.6 for sample Red Flags.

Red Flags are scored either for the teacher being observed or for the classroom (with the exception of Red Flag Item 8, which can be scored for *either* the individual

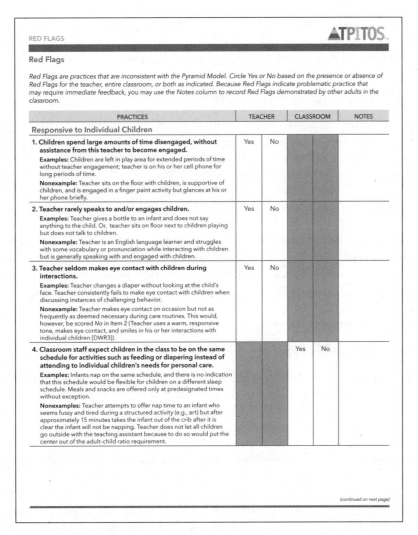

Figure 3.6. Sample Red Flag Items.

teacher *or* the classroom). Teacher Red Flags are Items that pertain to specific teacher practices and would be addressed specifically with the observed teacher. These Items address teacher responsivity, emotional expression, and social interaction and teacher response to children's distress and challenging behavior. For example, Red Flags include teachers rarely speaking to or making eye contact with children, using flat affect, or speaking harshly to children.

Red Flags that are scored for the classroom pertain to practices or policies that occur at the teaching team or classroom level, rather than related to individual teachers' practices. For example, classroom Red Flags include practices in which all children are expected to follow the classroom schedule, children in distress are left unattended, and environmental arrangements limit child engagement and interaction.

On occasions in which Red Flags are observed for a teacher *other than* the observed teacher (i.e., the assistant teacher or classroom aide), these incidents should be recorded in the notes column of the Red Flag section so that they can be addressed later. The space for you to record these concerns is provided because Red Flags are Items that are typically addressed immediately or very soon after the observation, and it is important to make note of them when they occur. Observers remain alert for Red Flags throughout the observation, score them as they occur, and then finalize Red Flag scoring after the observation is complete.

CONCLUDING THE OBSERVATION

After the observation, confirm with the teacher whether this observation period was typical of daily routines and interactions or whether there were unusual circumstances that may have affected the observation. Examples of circumstances that might have affected the observation could include having a new child in the classroom or having a substitute assistant teacher. Complete any remaining note taking to inform the scoring process. Refer to your notes frequently as you provide a score of *Yes*, *No*, or *N/A* for each Indicator. Review the TPITOS Scoring Form to ensure that you have completed all relevant observation and interview Items, as well as the Red Flags. Thank teachers for allowing you to observe and for the time to conduct the interview. It is also recommended that you keep your written notes from the observation for later reference. For instructions on obtaining summary scores, refer to Chapter 5.

RECOMMENDED TRAINING PROCEDURES BEFORE USING THE TPITOS

The TPITOS is a tool for measuring the fidelity with which teaching practices are implemented and requires training for reliable use. It is strongly recommended that individuals or groups of individuals from programs or agencies who would like to use the TPITOS in their program or as a coach become certified in use of the TPITOS. The certification process involves attending the TPITOS Reliability Training, conducted by a certified TPITOS Master Trainer who has been certified by the authors or approved as a TPITOS Trainer by the authors or publisher. It is important that observers who use the TPITOS become certified so that there is assurance that the TPITOS scoring of one observer is consistent with those of other TPITOS observers, as well as with the test developers and master trainers. When there are multiple observers within a program or center, it is particularly important for observers to become certified so that the scores obtained by one observer are comparable to the scores obtained by other observers. If two observers are using different criteria to score TPITOS Items, it becomes difficult to interpret those data or have confidence in the reliability of the data.

The prerequisites for attending the TPITOS Reliability Training and becoming a certified observer include having participated in professional development activities that focus on the *Pyramid Model* and the implementation of the *Pyramid Model* practices within infant and toddler classrooms. Users should have a thorough understanding of the *Pyramid Model* and its related infant and toddler practices prior to TPITOS Reliability Training. Completion of the Infant–Toddler Modules, developed by the Center on the Social and Emotional Foundations for Early Learning, is one example of how this prerequisite can be met.

TPITOS Reliability Training typically lasts 2 days. The first day involves an overview of the manual, training and practice scoring the Items, including procedures for scoring Observational Items, Interview Items, and Red Flags. Participants view brief practice videos and score teacher practices, comparing their scores to those of the trainer. On the second day, observers view a 2-hour classroom video recording and the subsequent teacher interview. Participants use this video and interview to score the TPITOS. Their scores are then compared with a master code to determine whether the minimum 80% interobserver agreement on TPITOS Items has been obtained. If observers do not reach 80% agreement during the training, the participant scores an additional video by working with the trainer remotely after the training session.

In addition to completing the TPITOS Reliability Training and obtaining 80% agreement with master TPITOS coders, we recommend users administer the measure in infant and toddler classrooms and compare their scores against those of other trained TPITOS users before administering the TPITOS independently. If the TPITOS is used to measure teacher fidelity or to guide professional development, we recommend that interobserver agreement checks are used to ensure that observers are using the tool in a consistent and reliable manner. To accomplish this, two observers conduct a TPITOS observation together, but independently. They then calculate the percentage of interobserver agreement by counting the number of Indicators that were scored with the same response and the total number of Indicators possible. The number of Indicators for which both observers agreed on the same score is divided by the total number of Items scored (Agreements/[Agreements + Disagreements]) and then multiplied by 100. This percentage score indicates the percentage of Indicators for which there was observer agreement out of the total number of Indicators scored and provides an Indicator of how observers are adhering to the assessment protocol. Furthermore, it is strongly recommended that observers conduct periodic interobserver reliability checks (i.e., annually). If the TPITOS will be administered within an organization by more than one individual, it is especially important to establish interobserver agreement with other observers within the organization. This is crucial to ensuring that TPITOS scores are comparable across observers and to correct observer drift or the gradual shifts that tend to occur over time in the way in which observers score Indicators. When conducting interobserver reliability observations, both observers should establish agreement about how the observation will be structured. For instance, two observers should agree on the specific time when each routine ends and the next begins (e.g., transitions from meal to play), but they should score TPITOS Indicators independently as a check of their reliability. Note that becoming reliable does not give observers permission to train others on use of the tool.

SUMMARY

In this chapter, we provided guidance on administration of the TPITOS, including conducting the observation and the interview, as well as the Red Flags. We discussed how TPITOS users should be trained in use of the measure. In the next chapter, we provide definitions of key terms and TPITOS Items and Indicators and additional scoring guidance.

CHAPTER 4

Teaching Pyramid Infant–Toddler Observation Scale Scoring Guidance

In this chapter, we provide definitions for key terms and definitions for each TPITOS Indicator and the Red Flags. The guidance provided should be used to determine whether the observed or reported practices should be scored as occurring or not occurring. Elaborations provide examples and nonexamples of practices associated with each indicator, but should not be considered an exhaustive list of the practices that would meet the scoring criteria for each indicator.

In general, we define the term *infants* as children between birth and 18 months of age. *Toddlers* are generally between the ages of 19 and 36 months. The terms *infants* and *toddlers* refer to these general age ranges, but it is understood that there are vast differences in developmental levels within those two age groupings, as well as among children of the same age within each of those groupings. Furthermore, any one classroom will have a range of ages represented, and those ranges will vary based on center policies, state policies, as well as the general makeup of the room. It is up to observers to use their understanding of the makeup of the classroom and the children present to make decisions about scoring.

KEY DEFINITIONS IN THE TPITOS

The following terms appear throughout the TPITOS. Observers should be familiar with these terms so that their interpretations are consistent with the authors' intentions.

Challenging behavior can occur in infant and toddler classrooms, but in many instances these behaviors can be considered common or typical among this age group. Tantrums, distress, physical aggression, biting, crying, taking toys from others, throwing objects, and noncompliance can be challenging behaviors, but in many cases these are not uncommon or unexpected for infants and toddlers. Thus, these behaviors can often be more accurately reframed as "challenging situations." For the purposes of TPITOS scoring, Items and Indicators referring to challenging behavior also apply to such challenging situations, and this has been indicated as such within the Indicators and Elaborations.

Distress is a persistent or prolonged state of upset, crying, or screaming that is loud or disruptive or interferes with the child's engagement in activities.

Dual language learner (DLL) is a term used to describe a child who is learning two (or more) languages, one of which is usually English.

Engagement refers to a child's active attending or participation in an activity. For example, a child is considered engaged when following directions, actively communicating or interacting with a peer or adult, or displaying focused attention to the activity, materials, or interaction.

Expectations are standards, communicated by adults, that a behavior or action should or should not happen in the future. These may be communicated in a number of ways, such as by stating rules, modeling appropriate behavior, providing feedback to children who are exhibiting appropriate behavior, guiding children's actions, or redirecting instances of an inappropriate behavior. For example, if a caregiver asks a toddler not to throw Cheerios on the floor at snack time, the caregiver is stating an expectation for the child to meet. Similarly, if a caregiver states the rule, "We use soft touches," this communicates another expectation.

Free play activities may include free choice of play activities or other activities in which there is no intentional or overt focus or goal initiated by the teacher. Play activities primarily include activities that are child initiated and directed rather than teacher initiated or directed. Play activities differ from structured group activities in that the teacher has not intentionally introduced a focus or objective to a particular activity or set of materials. Examples might include an activity in which children are free to choose an activity or toy from the set of toys available to the classroom or when children have free choice to move about the room between various play areas.

Infant is generally defined as a child from birth to 18 months of age.

Negative social interaction is undesired behavior directed at a peer or adult that may or may not be disruptive enough to be considered a challenging behavior. Examples include: 1) taking toys away from other children forcefully, 2) ordering an adult to do something (e.g., "leave me alone"), and 3) making statements that are noncompliant (e.g., "I'm not going to do it") or clear and explicit verbal or physical refusal to follow directions. In many cases, one instance of such a behavior might simply be considered a negative social interaction, whereas a pattern of such behaviors might be considered challenging behavior.

Outdoor activities are those that take place in outdoor areas or on the playground. When coding outdoor routines, this may also include activities that take place indoors in place of outdoor play. For instance, during inclement weather, the classroom moves to a large, indoor play area for gross motor activities. This would be coded as "outdoors." Moving to this same type of space for a craft could be considered "small group" activity.

Personal care routines are activities that focus on eating, diaper changing, toileting, dressing, teeth brushing, and hygiene (e.g., hand washing). Morning and afternoon pick-up and drop-off would be categorized as "care routines" and can be scored as part of this routine.

Structured group activities are those in which a teacher initiates or directs an activity and brings together two or more children to engage in this activity. In order to call an activity a "structured group activity," there is, generally, an intentional focus on a particular activity, objective, or set of materials, and there is some degree of planning that went into creating this activity. For example, circle time with a group of children, an art project led by the teacher, shared book reading with intentional teaching of vocabulary words, and a cooking activity involving mixing ingredients might all be structured group activities. An example of an activity that would not be designated as structured is one during which a child is playing with a toy and additional children join that child to play with that toy, but the teacher has not introduced a specific focus or objective. When it is not clear whether an activity would be categorized as a "free play" activity or "structured group" activity, use your best judgment based on the teacher's role in that activity and how it came about. Ultimately, this distinction is made just to help the observer in providing meaningful and specific feedback to the teacher.

Toddler is generally defined as a child aged 19–36 months.

Transition is a change in one classroom activity to another that includes one or more children and may or may not entail actual physical movement to a new location. For example, transitions may include moving from play to snack time or getting ready to clean up before going outside.

Variety, when used in the elaborations, is generally defined as at least two of the strategies or practices having been observed or reported.

TPITOS ITEMS

The following Elaborations are used as guidance in scoring TPITOS Item Indicators.

Item 1: Teacher Provides Opportunities for Communication and Building Relationships (CBR)

CBR1.   Teacher talks often to individual children.

To score *Yes*, the teacher talks about the activities in which the child is engaged or in which they are engaged together (e.g., cleaning up playdough). A verbal response from the child is not required, particularly for younger infants. For infants, this might involve the teacher talking about what he or she is doing during a diaper change. For toddlers, this might involve back-and-forth conversations, but this is not required. For toddlers, a teacher might use more open-ended questions and allow more opportunities for the child to respond. For a younger infant, the teacher might "narrate" a child's actions or supply answers to questions asked. Talk should be appropriate to the context and to young children in general. Score *No* if the teacher does not talk to the children or if talk is minimal.

CBR2.   Teacher joins in children's activities and follows the child's lead by matching the focus of his or her attention to the child's focus of attention.

To score *Yes*, when engaged in joint activities the teacher aligns his or her focus of attention with the child rather than imposing a new focus in the activity. For example, when a child talks about the food that barnyard animals eat while he or she is playing with a barn and farm animals, the teacher follows the child's lead in talking about food or how the animals eat and does not change the topic to talk about other topics. Younger infants may be less likely to be actively engaged in an independent activity. A teacher might notice what the infant is looking at and talk about that. For an older toddler looking at books, the teacher might identify what is on the page. Score *No* if the teacher does not follow the child's lead, frequently talks about topics that are not aligned with the child's interest, or frequently attempts to change the child's focus of attention when the child is engaged in an appropriate activity.

CBR3.   Teacher comments on children's interests, activities, or actions.

Score *Yes* if the teacher talks about, names, labels, or elaborates on the activities in which children are engaged, the materials they are using, or the focus of their attention.

Examples of commenting include labeling a child's actions (e.g., "You're jumping so high.") or naming an activity in which the teacher and child are engaged together (e.g., "We are building a tall tower."). For younger infants, the teacher might talk about the toy the child is holding. With a toddler, the teacher might name the foods, and different aspects of the food (e.g., sweet, sour, the color) at lunch time. Score *No* if the teacher does not talk about the child's interests.

CBR4. Teacher imitates and/or expands upon children's vocalizations or imitates actions.

Score *Yes* if the teacher imitates an infant's vocalizations or rephrases something a toddler says in a different or grammatically correct form. The teacher might elaborate on what the child says by providing some additional information to the child's utterance. For a younger infant, this might involve imitating babies' cooing or babbling sounds. For toddlers, teachers might imitate words or sentences or expand on them by providing additional information (e.g., after a child says "bunny," the teacher says, "Yes, that's a brown bunny. It looks like she's hopping."). This may also include imitating actions, such as imitating clapping, waving or pointing, or playing peek-a-boo. Score *No* if the teacher does not imitate actions or imitate or expand on a child's vocalizations in any way.

CBR5. Teacher listens and responds to children's attempts to communicate.

Score *Yes* if the teacher engages in active listening when children are talking or attempting to communicate, is patient, allows children to complete utterances, and responds to attempts to communicate. For infants, the teacher might listen for babbling and then respond by making eye contact and imitating the child's utterance. For a toddler, the teacher responds to child's initiations, and contributes to a back-and-forth conversation with the child. Score *No* if the teacher does not listen and respond to child communication.

CBR6. Teacher encourages child communication, skills, behaviors, and activities through positive, descriptive statements.

Score *Yes* if the teacher makes positive, descriptive statements aimed at encouraging and supporting child communication and behavior. Statements should be more than a simple, "Good job!" or similar statement. The teacher describes the child's actions in a positive, descriptive manner (e.g., "You're really using soft touches with Lakeisha."). This might also involve statements such as, "I like how you are being such a good friend," or "I like how you are using your words." Score *No* if the teacher does not use positive, descriptive statements.

CBR7. Teacher provides opportunities for children to initiate social interactions and provides time throughout interactions for the child to take a turn or form a response.

Score *Yes* if throughout interactions with children, the teacher provides multiple opportunities for children to initiate exchanges or conversations and provides time to respond. This would include pausing or waiting quietly to allow time for a response and listening and responding appropriately throughout interactions to encourage child initiations. For example, while reading a story, the teacher pauses periodically to allow children to contribute to the conversation. When a teacher is talking about current activities, he or she pauses occasionally so children can take a turn or respond. Score *No* if the teacher fails to provide opportunities for children to initiate or respond during interactions.

CBR8. Teacher uses alternative strategies for communicating with children who have language delays or are DLLs.

Engaging with children with disabilities or language delays or who are DLLs may require teachers to use different modes of communication. Supportive communication interactions with a child with a disability or delay may look different from interactions with a child who does not have a disability or delay. These interactions may be different in content and may involve simpler language, shorter phrases, or fewer back-and-forth turns. Examples of alternative communication strategies may include but are not limited to sign language, conventional gestures, or pictures. A teacher might use the child's primary or home language or speak in simpler sentences. Score *No* if the teacher does not employ alternative strategies when children who have language delays or are DLLs are present. Mark *N/A* if children who have language delays or are DLLs are not enrolled.

Figure 4.1 illustrates Item 1 Indicators from the TPITOS Scoring Form.

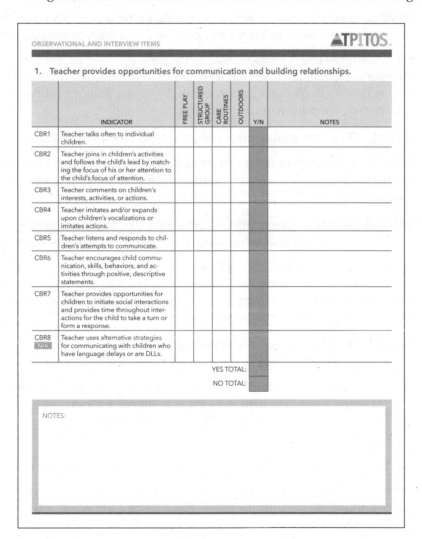

Figure 4.1. Item 1. Teacher provides opportunities for communication and building relationships (CBR).

Item 2: Teacher Demonstrates
Warmth and Responsivity to Individual Children (DWR)

**DWR1.   Teacher's tone toward the class is
generally positive, calm, and supportive.**

Score *Yes* if the teacher maintains a calm demeanor throughout interactions with all children. Tone is positive overall, and her basic interactions with children are supportive. Score *No* if the teacher's tone is harsh or negative.

**DWR2.   Teacher positions self at child's level
during interactions almost all of the time.**

Score *Yes* if the teacher communicates with children face-to-face and at eye level, spends time on the floor, or sits with the children at the table. The teacher is seldom seen standing and looking down when communicating with children. Score *No* if the teacher maintains a distance from children or continually stands while children are sitting on the floor.

**DWR3.   Teacher uses a warm, responsive tone, makes eye contact,
and smiles in his or her interactions with individual children.**

Score *Yes* if the teacher smiles, makes frequent eye contact, and uses kind words and phrases to individual children during interactions and activities and especially when they appear to need reassurance. Score *No* if you do not observe warmth, frequent eye contact, and smiles toward children.

DWR4.   Teacher shows physical affection toward children.

Score *Yes* if the teacher demonstrates affection for children by cuddling infants, hugging or holding children, holding their hands, or patting them gently. Score *No* if you observe no or very limited physical affection.

**DWR5.   Teacher greets and acknowledges children warmly
on arrival and whenever they enter an activity or area.**

Score *Yes* if the teacher acknowledges children's arrival at the beginning of the day and whenever they enter an activity or area. Teacher also refers to children often by name. Score *No* if you see limited evidence that the teacher greets or acknowledges children on arrival or throughout the day.

**DWR6.   Teacher shows a sincere interest
in children and is patient with children's initiations.**

Score *Yes* if the teacher takes time to listen to individual children and frequently responds to what they say with elaborations, questions, or comments. Score *No* if the teacher does not show evidence of listening to or show a sincere interest in children's initiations.

DWR7.   Teacher readily participates in children's play or activities.

Score *Yes* if the teacher joins in play or other activities with children, such as by playing with materials on the floor, participating in an art activity, reading books, or playing musical instruments with children. Score *No* if the teacher rarely joins in

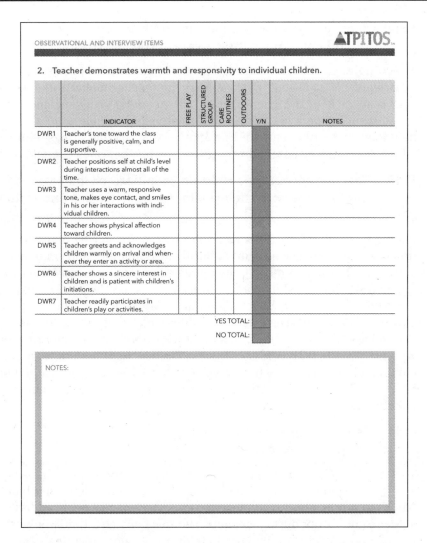

Figure 4.2.   Item 2. Teacher demonstrates warmth and responsivity to individual children (DWR).

children's play or when he or she is physically present but not actively participating in activities (i.e., teacher is on the floor with children but looking at his or her phone or talking with other teachers).

Figure 4.2 illustrates Item 2 Indicators from the TPITOS Scoring Form.

Item 3: Teacher Promotes Positive Peer Interactions (PPI)

PPI1.   Teacher remains nearby during children's social interactions.

To score *Yes,* the teacher should be in proximity of children during child-to-child exchanges for a majority of the time observed. Score *NO* if the teacher spends a majority time overseeing interactions between toddlers from a distance during outdoor play, for example.

PPI2.   Teacher encourages children to be aware of and care about their peers in the classroom.

To score *Yes*, you should witness the teacher intentionally bringing attention to a peer who is present or absent. For example, the teacher makes toddlers aware that their peer is out sick, or the teacher might help a toddler provide comfort to a peer who is upset about losing a pet. Score *No* if the teacher is clearly missing opportunities to help toddlers learn to care for one another (e.g., a child brings a toy to another child who is upset during parent drop-off, and the teacher does not acknowledge this).

PPI3.   Teacher encourages children to initiate or maintain interactions with their peers during activities and routines.

To score *Yes*, you should see at least two occasions of the teacher helping children initiate/maintain interactions with their peers. For instance, the teacher might position two infants to face each other during feeding times and comment on each other's activities. The teacher might point out when one infant is crawling toward another infant and say, "I think she's coming over to see you." The teacher helps a child playing alone with large blocks understand that an approaching, curious peer would like to play blocks with her. The teacher provides suggestions (e.g., "tap Jenny on the shoulder and ask if you can play") to a child who has difficultly entering a group of peers who are playing with cars and trucks. The teacher encourages a child to get other children involved in an activity (e.g., teacher suggests Ben take the book to Annie). Score *No* if you see fewer than two instances of the teacher helping a child initiate/maintain an interaction with a peer.

PPI4.   Teacher helps <u>toddlers</u> work cooperatively during activities/routines.

To score *Yes*, you should see the teacher provide toddlers with ideas as to how they can work together. For example, a teacher suggests one toddler hand another child blocks to put in a basket at cleanup time. The teacher helps a toddler give a doll to a peer to put away during cleanup. The teacher helps toddlers work together with Legos to build a dragon by giving children assigned roles (e.g., one child is the tail builder, and another one is the piece finder). Score *No* if instances of toddlers working cooperatively together are stopped by the teacher (e.g., children are making a boat together with playdough and the teacher directs them to work with the playdough by themselves) or when the majority of opportunities to help children work cooperatively are missed by the teacher. Score *N/A* if there are no toddlers present.

PPI5.   Teacher provides positive descriptive comments to children who are engaging in positive peer interactions.

To score *Yes*, you should hear the teacher support peer-to-peer interactions through positive statements on two occasions. For example, the teacher tells a toddler, "You did a good job sharing the blocks" when sharing of this classroom material occurs. The teacher provides a positive statement to infants who are both playing with an activity box (e.g., "He sees you smiling, and he likes it."). The teacher tells toddlers they are doing a great job taking turns running through the sprinkler. Teacher describes a toddler's positive behavior toward another (e.g., "Celia, you handed Danny a block so he could finish his tower"). Score *No* if the teacher fails to acknowledge a child's positive behavior toward a peer on two occasions.

PPI6.   Teacher offers comfort when negative social interactions occur among children.

To score *Yes*, the teacher should be attentive to negative toddler-to-toddler interactions and provide comfort when these incidents occur. For example, a teacher provides reassurance to a toddler after a challenging interaction through calming words. The teacher holds a toddler after she is hit by a peer during snack. The teacher helps a toddler rebuild a tower that was knocked down by a peer who refuses to help. Score *No* if there are prolonged instances of children interacting negatively toward each other without teacher intervention. Score *N/A* if there are no negative social interactions observed.

PPI7.   Teacher models social skills for children, such as sharing, gentle touching, requesting, or using words.

To score *Yes*, the teacher should model important social skills for the early childhood classroom. For instance, a teacher might model how a child can request a toy from another child (e.g., "I am going to let Jeremy play with my doll because he asked nicely.") and how a child in possession of a toy can agree/not agree to share (e.g., "We'll tell Marie she can have the doll when the timer rings, if you're still playing with it."). A teacher may model smiling, waving, and saying "hello" when greeting visitors to the room or demonstrate how to hand a toy to another child. The teacher shows a child how to rub another child's back who is upset about having to go down for a nap. Score *No* if the teacher does not take the opportunity to model appropriate social skill(s). Score *N/A* if modeling was not the appropriate strategy.

PPI8.   Teacher helps children understand their peers' intentions.

Score *Yes* when a teacher helps a child understand a peer's emotions or actions (e.g., "I think Meyer wants to play with you. He is pointing to your ball."). Score *No* if the teacher does not help children understand their peers' intentions, or if a majority of the teacher's language related to toddler-to-toddler interactions is directive/instructive (e.g., "Go give the ball to Meyer.").

PPI9.   Teacher uses a variety (i.e., more than one) of developmentally appropriate strategies and/or materials (e.g., books, puppets) to encourage peer-to-peer interactions (OBS/INT).

To score *Yes*, you should observe the teacher supporting child-to-child positive interactions through a variety of strategies and/or materials, such as making positive comments about peer interactions, encouraging interactions through songs, using books to introduce social skills, or using puppets to model social interactions. The teacher uses a puppet show to demonstrate how toddlers should respond when pushed by a friend or model greetings (e.g., saying "hi" and waving) for infants. The teacher might structure a play routine in which children take turns and exchange materials, and emphasize turn-taking in a game or craft. Score *No* if materials that can support children's peer relations are available and the teacher does not make use of them or does not use a variety of strategies or materials for encouraging interaction.

Figure 4.3 illustrates Item 3 Indicators from the TPITOS Scoring Form.

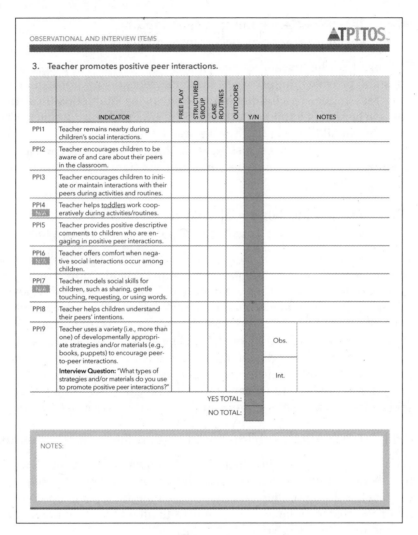

Figure 4.3.   Item 3. Teacher promotes positive peer interactions (PPI).

Item 4: Teacher Promotes Children's Active Engagement (CAE)

CAE1.   Teacher makes positive and varied attempts to encourage unengaged children to become engaged in an activity.

The teacher helps all children in the class become engaged in activities or interactions through visual or verbal prompting, modeling, providing developmentally appropriate activities/materials, or physically supporting children in playing with or using materials. "Developmentally appropriate" refers to activities that are appropriate for the diversity of children's ages, developmental levels, and interests. Score *Yes* if the teacher is observed introducing a new activity, initiating an interaction, or providing prompts, or if the teacher is observed supporting an unengaged infant or toddler in manipulating or exploring materials. For example, this might involve moving a toy in closer proximity to the child or shaking a toy so it makes noise, in an attempt to increase interest. If all children are engaged in activities throughout the observation, you can assume children are receiving the support they need and can score a *Yes*.

Score *No* if you see unengaged children and the teacher does not initiate one or more attempts to engage children.

CAE2.   Teacher uses a variety of ways to help children sustain their engagement in an activity.

Score *Yes* if the teacher is observed adjusting an activity, such as by introducing novelty or making slight changes to the activity or by using a variety of prompts to re-engage a child who might have become disengaged. For example, a teacher might follow the lead of an infant who is engaged with a squeaky toy and then prompt her to continue engaging the squeaky toy through following the child's lead in talking about the toy or providing verbal or visual prompts. A teacher might also demonstrate how a toy can be used in a slightly different way or add a new object to a play activity in order to sustain a child's engagement. With a toddler, a teacher might help a child sustain engagement by scaffolding the child's engagement by adding new actions or words to what a child is already doing in the activity or making comments or asking questions that might lead a child to explore objects in a slightly different manner. Score *No* if the teacher shows no evidence of using a variety of ways to sustain engagement in an activity.

CAE3.   Teacher provides attention and positive comments to children who are engaged in activities or with materials.

Score *Yes* if the teacher is observed attending, talking with, or playing with children who are actively engaged in classroom activities or materials in a given routine. To be scored *Yes*, you would observe at least two positive comments in one routine. Score *No* if attention and positive comments to engaged children are never or rarely observed.

CAE4.   Teacher provides <u>toddlers</u> with opportunities to make choices.

Score *Yes* if the teacher provides a child or multiple children with at least two choices during the routine observed. Choices should be provided in an explicit manner and not simply be an array of options made available to children. For example, score *Yes* if a teacher says, "Francisco, do you want peaches or melon for snack today?" or, "Here are two books we could read. Which would you like?" Score *No* if choices were offered fewer than two times by the teacher. Also score *No* if the teacher simply makes a variety of materials or books available to children or simply asks, "Do you want this?" without offering an explicit choice of at least two items (i.e., teacher sets out a bin of toys). Score *N/A* if no toddlers are present.

CAE5.   Adults in the room work together to make sure all children are engaged (OBS/INT).

Score *Yes* if you observe at least one example of the teacher helping another teacher/ teachers to make sure all children are engaged. For example, if a teacher is occupied with a large group and one child appears to need some help becoming engaged, the teacher either calls for assistance, or another teacher comes to the aid of the teacher to help support the child in need. In the interview, a teacher would indicate how the teachers coordinate to keep all children engaged. Score *No* if there are no observed examples and if the interview does not yield evidence of how the classroom staff work together to ensure that all children are engaged. Score *N/A* if only one teacher is present.

Figure 4.4 illustrates Item 4 Indicators from the TPITOS Scoring Form.

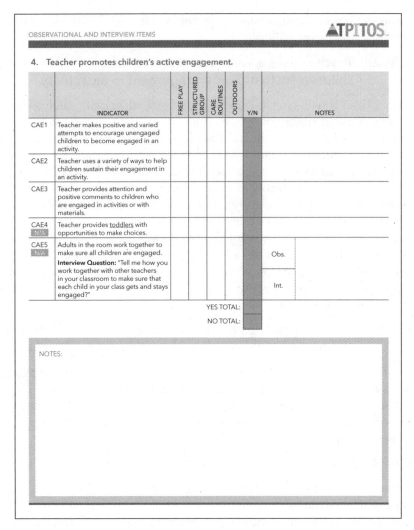

Figure 4.4. Item 4. Teacher promotes children's active engagement (CAE).

Item 5: Teacher Is Responsive to Children's Expression of Emotions and Teaches About Feelings (REF)

> **REF1.   Teacher demonstrates understanding of children's feelings and provides labels for how children are feeling.**

Score *Yes* if the teacher picks up on various emotional states of the child (e.g., happy, frustrated, angry, scared) and provides a label for the feeling. For infants, this might involve labeling emotions for a crying infant (e.g., "Oh, are you feeling sad?"). For a toddler, teachers might label more complex emotions (e.g., "You seem frustrated, Mario," "Our friends are curious," or "I am so proud."). Score *No* if the teacher typically ignores children's expressions of feelings.

> **REF2.   Teacher asks questions about and/or offers expansions related to children's emotions.**

Score *Yes* if you see the teacher asking questions about children's emotions. (e.g., "Mario, are you FRUSTRATED because you can't get anything out of the bottle?"

"Alicia, you fell on your bottom—did that SCARE you?"). These expansions might be more complex for a toddler than for an infant. Score *No*, if you see children who are clearly demonstrating some emotional response and you never see the teacher inquiring about how they might be feeling.

REF3.   Teacher points out peers' words, voice tone, or facial expressions to help <u>toddlers</u> recognize and understand emotions.

Score *Yes* if you see teachers pointing out emotional expressions of their peers and using that to help toddlers recognize and understand emotions (e.g., "Look, Ben is happy. He's smiling because his Momma is here," "Milo is crying. He's sad," or "It sounds like Eli is getting frustrated trying to use the scissors."). Score *No* if you do not observe a teacher pointing out children's words, voice tone, or facial expression to help children understand their peers' emotions or if the majority of opportunities to help toddlers recognize and understand peers' emotions are missed. Score *N/A* if no toddlers are present.

REF4.   Teacher uses opportunities during activities to teach about feelings.

Score *Yes* if you observe a teacher embedding feeling words into everyday classroom activities (e.g., during make-believe play, talks about feelings; during stories, asks about how characters are feeling). For example, while playing with action figures and acting out a scenario, the teacher uses this opportunity to label a character's emotions in that scenario (e.g., "He sees his friend. I think he is happy."). Score *No* if you see no instances in which teachers refer to or talk about feelings during classroom activities or if the majority of opportunities to teach about feelings are missed.

REF5.   Teacher labels own emotions in response to real-life classroom situations.

Score *Yes* if you observe the teacher labeling his or her own emotions in relation to real-life classroom situations (e.g., "I'm feeling frustrated, so I'd better take some deep breaths," or "I'm sad that we can't go outside because it's so cold."). The emotions being labeled should be related to classroom activities in some manner, rather than personal teacher situations (e.g., "I'm so upset my phone is broken"). Score *No* if the teacher does not label his or her own emotions in relation to classroom activities.

REF6.   Teacher uses real-life classroom situations to identify feelings and problem-solve when <u>toddlers</u> have conflicts or when <u>toddlers</u> experience frustration.

Teacher uses real-life conflict situations to identify feelings and model or practice age-appropriate problem-solving with toddlers. For example, if a toddler becomes frustrated with a puzzle, the teacher says, "I see you're frustrated—that's a tough puzzle. You can ask me for help when you are frustrated. I can help you." Score *Yes* if you see teachers use conflict situations to teach social skills by modeling problem-solving strategies (e.g., how children can share materials) while using words to describe the behavior. Score *No* if the teacher does not take the opportunity to help toddlers identify feelings and demonstrate problem-solving strategies when conflicts or frustrations arise or when the majority of opportunities to use real-life situations to help toddlers identify feelings and problem solve are missed. Score *N/A* if there are no situations in which this could be scored or there are no toddlers present.

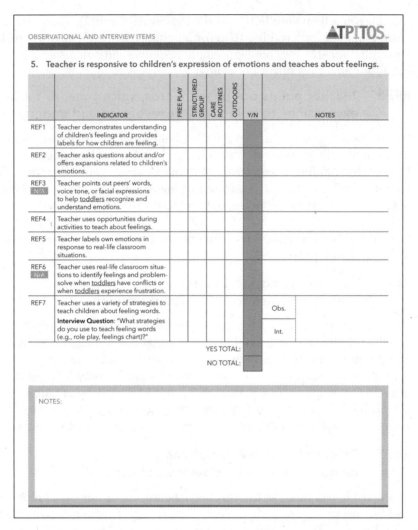

Figure 4.5. Item 5. Teacher is responsive to children's expression of emotions and teaches about feelings (REF).

REF7. Teacher uses a variety of strategies to teach children about feeling words (OBS/INT).

Teacher uses strategies to teach feeling words that are varied and/or uses them across a variety of activities or situations. Score *Yes* if the teacher introduces feeling words using a variety of strategies, such as through labeling emotions, reading books about feelings, doing art projects that address feelings, discussing feelings during circle time, or modeling talking about their own emotions. Score *No* if the teacher does not talk or teach about feeling words in a variety of ways.

Figure 4.5 illustrates Item 5 Indicators from the TPITOS Scoring Form.

Item 6. Teacher Communicates and Provides Feedback About Developmentally Appropriate Behavioral Expectations (CBE)

If during the observation, the teacher has not explicitly communicated expectations, rely on what would be appropriate for the age group being observed.

CBE1.   Teacher expectations are developmentally appropriate and individualized as needed.

Teachers have developmentally appropriate expectations that are specific to infants (e.g., infants are allowed to put toys in their mouths) and toddlers (e.g., toddlers are encouraged to use hands as opposed to mouths to explore toys). Score *Yes* if the teacher allows a younger toddler who is having trouble sitting still to move around during story time or allows toddlers to play independently while others are engaged in a group activity. Additional examples include encouraging toddlers to use crayons or markers, with the expectation that they may not hold them correctly. They are encouraged to hold them correctly, but it is not required. If the teacher has toddler-age expectations of infants (e.g., infants are told not to chew on books), then mark *No*.

CBE2.   Teacher communicates behavioral expectations by letting <u>toddlers</u> know, in a positive tone, what they should do in specific activities (and not just what they shouldn't do.)

Score *Yes* if the teacher communicates expectations in a positive tone. For example, before free play begins, toddlers are provided specific examples as to how to play nicely with friends. Teachers explain that in order to ride tricycles during outdoor play time, they will need to take turns. The teacher tells toddlers that after snack they will need to go wash their hands. If the teacher only focuses on what <u>not</u> to do (e.g., "Remember, we don't hit each other."), then score *No*. Score *N/A* if no toddlers are present.

CBE3.   Teacher demonstrates behavioral expectations in specific activities through modeling.

Score *Yes* if the teacher models behavioral expectations. For example, in teaching about holding hands when walking down the hall, the teacher might say, "Find your buddy's hand and hold onto it" and then gently reach out to hold onto one of the toddler's hands. The teacher models for infants how to put toys in a bin during cleanup time. The teacher demonstrates what "walking feet" looks like or how to have soft touches with peers. Score *No* if the teacher does not model behavior associated with child behavioral expectations.

CBE4.   Teacher frequently acknowledges, praises, and/or encourages appropriate behavior related to expectations.

Score *Yes* if the teacher provides positive, specific feedback to toddlers about their behavior and its relationship to classroom expectations. For example, the teacher might say, "When you put the cups on the table for snack, you were being very helpful"—the classroom expectation in this case would be "being helpful." The teacher praises an older infant who puts the book back on the shelf after story time. The teacher encourages a toddler to use gentle touching with friends and then acknowledges this behavior by stating, "You are using such soft touches. That's being a good friend." As with indicator CBE2, this would be scored *No* if the teacher provides feedback that is negative more often than positive.

CBE5.   Teacher uses simple words or phrases to explain natural consequences of engaging in unsafe behavior.

Score *Yes* if the teacher uses simple words or phrases to explain natural consequences when toddlers engage in behavior that is unsafe for themselves or peers, such as climbing on tall furniture or playing with a toy in a manner that could injure another child. For instance, "If you climb up the cabinet, you could fall and hurt yourself," or "If you swing that around, it might hurt your friends." Score *No* if unsafe behavior is observed but the teacher does not talk about the natural consequences of such behavior. Mark *N/A* if unsafe behavior is not observed.

CBE6. Teacher provides feedback to <u>toddlers</u> in instances of behavior that does not meet classroom expectations.

Score *Yes* if overall teacher physical and verbal responses are both gentle and appropriate when teachers provide feedback to toddlers on behavior that does not meet expectations. For example, if a toddler grabs the teacher's hair, she lightly ungrasps the child's fingers and then tells the child in a calm voice that pulling her hair hurts and we should use soft touches. The teacher helps two boys who were throwing water at each other during hand-washing time understand appropriate behaviors for this routine. When toddlers are not assisting with cleanup, the teacher reminds children that when the lights go off and the cleanup song starts, then it is time to cleanup. Mark *No* if the teacher consistently scolds the child in instances where behavioral expectations are not met. Mark *N/A* if there are no instances of behavior not meeting classroom expectations or there are no toddlers present.

CBE7. Teacher anticipates potential conflict situations or instances in which behavior may not meet classroom expectations and provides guidance to children before the situations get out of control (OBS/INT).

Score *Yes* if the teacher uses or reports using strategies aimed at anticipating and preventing conflicts between children, such as providing duplicate toys so that all children in a small play group have their own toys or if multiple toys are available in a play area to ensure that all children in the play area have their own materials. Other examples might include limiting the number of children in a play station (e.g., only three children allowed in the house area at a time). This might also involve talking through potentially challenging situations with children to prevent conflict, such as reminding children how they might share or take turns while playing. Score *No* if the teacher does not take steps to anticipate and avoid conflict or challenging situations (i.e., there are not enough materials available for the children present) or if the teacher appears to notice or observe conflict and does not address it. Also score *No* if the teacher does not describe examples of this practice, if scored based on interview items.

Figure 4.6 illustrates Item 6 Indicators from the TPITOS Scoring Form.

Item 7. Teacher Responds to Children in Distress and Manages Challenging Behaviors (RDC)

RDC1. Teacher's tone remains calm, supportive, and positive during children's distressful or challenging episodes.

Score *Yes* if overall the teacher's physical and verbal responses are both gentle and appropriate during distressing/challenging situations or when challenging behavior occurs. For example, if two children are in conflict over a toy and both children are crying, the teacher calmly and gently provides a duplicate toy, attempts to engage them in a new activity, and talks about how they can play together. Mark *No* if the teacher scolds the child in instances where behavioral expectations are not met or does not remain calm, supportive, and positive. Score *N/A* if there are no instances of child distress, challenging situations, or challenging behavior.

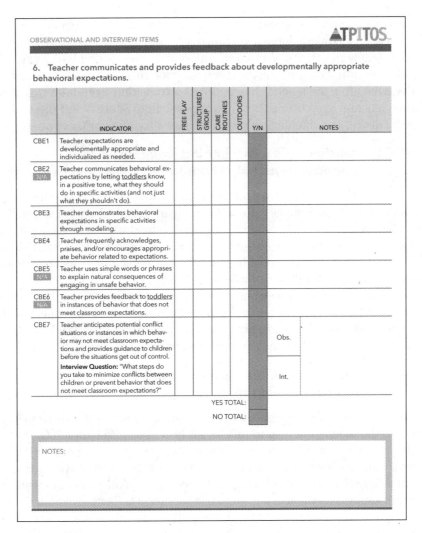

Figure 4.6. Item 6. Teacher communicates and provides feedback about developmentally appropriate behavioral expectations (CBE).

RDC2. Teacher immediately responds to children in distress to assess children's status.

Score *Yes* if children who are upset are responded to quickly by the teacher in a positive verbal and/or physical manner (i.e., moving close to the child to assess the situation). For example, when an infant drops a bottle on the ground and begins to cry, the teacher steps in quickly and helps the child calm down. Score *N/A* if there are no instances of child distress. If the teacher ignores toddlers who are in distress for any lengthy period of time (e.g., longer than a few minutes or what seems appropriate to the situation given safety concerns and the context), mark *No*—clear cases of planned ignoring, in which the teacher is consciously choosing to not reinforce or attend to an undesirable behavior, would be an exception.

RDC3. Teacher provides positive attention to toddlers when they have calmed down and are behaving appropriately.

Positive attention might include talking with the toddler about the day's activities, welcoming the toddler back to the group, playing with the toddler, or giving a quick hug.

Score *Yes* if the teacher waits to provide positive reinforcement to the toddler (e.g., "You did a good job taking three deep breaths.") after a tantrum ended, for example. Score *No* if the teacher provides positive attention when the toddler is still engaging in undesired behavior. For example, the child is having a tantrum because he wants another ride on the trike after the teacher has initiated a transition from bike riding, and the teacher then lets him keep riding simply to appease him. Score *N/A* if there are no instances of child distress or challenging behavior among toddlers or there are no toddlers present.

RDC4. Teacher uses a challenging situation as an opportunity to help children recognize and deal with emotions.

If a situation occurs where a toddler is angry because another child took her toy, for example, the teacher might help that child learn and understand words that describe that feeling. A teacher might help children understand what it means to be sad when a child has challenges at morning drop-off and misses a parent when he or she leaves for work. To score *Yes*, a teacher would help the child understand the feeling and help teach a label for that feeling. Another example is the teacher helping a toddler who is upset about not being able to play a game where there are no open "spots" talk through why he or she is so upset. Score *No* if teacher avoids addressing the emotional aspect of challenging situations or addresses them in a harsh or insensitive manner. Score *N/A* if there are no opportunities to observe how the teacher uses challenging situations as a teaching opportunity.

RDC5. Teacher provides support to <u>toddlers</u> who are angry or upset to help them with problem solving, when appropriate.

With this indicator, the teacher works with the child not only to help the child understand the feeling but also to talk about how the child handled the situation (i.e., what the child did correctly and what the child could do differently in the future), which is how it differs from RCD4. Score *Yes* if a teacher has a back-and-forth conversation with a toddler related to hitting a peer who took one of his or her goldfish, for example. Another example is the teacher helping a toddler who is upset about the computer center being full talk through why he or she is upset and then helps the child identify options (e.g., going to another center until a space opens in computers). Score *N/A* if there are no instances of child distress or challenging behavior or there are no toddlers present.

RDC6. Teacher uses strategies such as redirection and/or planned ignoring with individual <u>toddlers</u> who are in distress or engage in occasional episodes of challenging behavior (OBS/INT).

Score *Yes* if you observe the teacher attempting to calmly use redirection and/or planned ignoring (e.g., consciously choosing to not reinforce or attend to an undesirable behavior) in response to distress or challenging behavior. Examples of effective strategies for handling in-the-moment challenges include redirection and subsequent praise (when child begins demonstrating desirable behavior), reiterating the rules/expectations in a calm voice, and ignoring minor challenging behavior while redirecting a child to more appropriate behavior. If you observe the teacher ignoring challenging behavior and then offering to play a game that excites the child once the challenging behavior stops, a *Yes* on this indicator would be in order. If a toddler is upset because there is no room at the sensory table and the teacher directs one of the toddler's peers to leave the area so that the toddler in distress has a place, then score *No*, because the teacher is actually supporting undesirable behavior. Score *N/A* if there are no instances of child distress, challenging situations, or challenging behavior or when there are no toddlers present.

RDC7. Teacher uses a variety of strategies to console, soothe, or calm children who are in distress and individualizes responses according to children and situations (OBS/INT).

Score *Yes* when the teacher introduces or teaches strategies aimed at helping console or calm children in distressing situations in a variety of ways. One strategy a teacher might use to help a toddler calm down would be the Tucker the Turtle technique (i.e., step 1: recognize the feeling; step 2: think "stop" and keep my hands to myself; step 3: tuck inside my "shell" and take three deep breaths; and step 4: come out when calm and think of a solution). Other strategies might include rocking an infant who is upset during drop-off, offering to read a book as a transition for a toddler who is refusing to lie down and becoming upset at nap/rest time, and talking to the child about reading quietly while other children are napping. Score *No* if the teacher does not use a variety of strategies in response to children who are upset or in distress or if the teacher uses the same strategy in all situations. Score *N/A* if there are no instances of child distress.

Figure 4.7 illustrates Item 7 Indicators from the TPITOS Scoring Form.

Figure 4.7. Item 7. Teacher responds to children in distress and manages challenging behaviors (RDC).

Item 8. Teacher Uses Specific Strategies or Modifications for Children with Disabilities/Delays or Who Are DLLs (SMD)

SMD1. **Teacher uses or reports using specific strategies or modifications to support the social-emotional development of children with disabilities/delays (OBS/INT).**

Score *Yes* when the teacher uses/reports strategies to support the social-emotional development of children with disabilities or delays. Examples might be incorporating sign language into the classroom, taking extra time to support a child during transition times, using visual schedules, simplifying a task, or using an augmentative or alternative communication (AAC) device. Score *No* if the teacher does not introduce modifications with children with disabilities or delays or does not report instances in which he or she introduces modifications during the interview. Score *N/A* if there are no children who require specific modifications.

SMD2. **Teacher uses or reports using specific strategies or modifications to promote social-emotional development with children who are DLLs (OBS/INT).**

Score *Yes* if, for a DLL, a teacher speaks to that child in his or her native language or signs with a child who is learning signing. Another example would be the use of a visual schedule. If more than one language is spoken by children in the room, the teacher should note how she uses strategies or modifications with at least two different children. Score *No* if the teacher does not introduce modifications with children who are DLLs, or the teacher does not report modifications in the interview. Score *N/A* if there are no children who require specific modifications with regard to dual languages.

Figure 4.8 illustrates Item 8 Indicators from the TPITOS Scoring Form.

Item 9. Teacher Conveys Predictability Through Carefully Planned Schedule, Routines, and Transitions (SRT)

SRT1. **A schedule is posted that describes the daily activities for the entire class.**

Score *Yes* if a written or visual schedule is displayed on the wall that provides information on the general sequence of daily activities for the children in the classroom and the approximate time that the activity will take place. Typical activities will include free play, snack and mealtimes, outdoor times, and so forth. Only general times and activities need to be displayed, with the understanding that the schedule will vary depending on classroom and individual child variables. Pictorial or object schedules are acceptable as well—the purpose is to demonstrate that all teachers in the room have a general schedule from which to work. Mark *No* if you see no sign of a schedule with daily activities and approximate times for daily activities.

SRT2. **Teacher follows the classroom schedule for the group but varies it when necessary to meet the needs of individual children.**

Score *Yes*, if the teacher shows evidence of planning activities for individual children to align with each child's own personal schedule, for infants in particular. For example, the teacher provides story time for a tired infant, while allowing others to engage in more active play. Mark *No* if it appears that the teacher expects infants to be diapered or nap at specific times and fails to respond to cues that the child might have these needs at a different time.

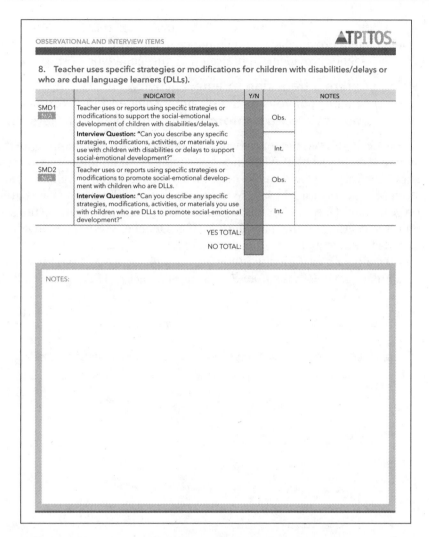

Figure 4.8. Item 8. Teacher uses specific strategies or modifications for children with disabilities/delays, or who are dual language learners (SMD).

SRT3. During group transitions for <u>toddlers</u>, teacher uses verbal and/or visual cues and a predictable routine that minimizes excessive waiting.

Score *Yes* if the teacher uses a transitional song, rhyme, saying, or activity (e.g., dimming the lights) to alert children to group transition, or other supports are in place that support group transitions and/or reduces waiting time. Mark *No* if there are group transitions but no transition signal, or if there is excessive waiting time (e.g., several minutes without an attempt to reduce waiting time or engage children). Mark *N/A* if you do not see group transitions or if there are no toddlers present.

SRT4. Teacher provides individualized support for children during transitions, providing visual/verbal cues or physical guidance as needed.

Score *Yes* if you see the teacher providing different types of support to children in the class who are functioning at different levels. For example, a teacher might provide a prompt to one child to throw out the trash after snack, but for another child the teacher might provide hands-on guidance in throwing out trash. Mark *No* if it appears that the teacher provides all children with the same type of support for transitions.

SRT5.   Before a transition to a new activity, teacher conveys in developmentally and individually appropriate ways information about what <u>toddlers</u> should expect.

Score *Yes* if you see the teacher telling toddlers what will happen next and providing simple directions about what they are supposed to do in the next activity. Directions should be very brief and can be conveyed by using words or visuals as appropriate. For example, a teacher might say, "When we're done washing hands, go to the circle and sit on your mat." Or a teacher might show a visual schedule showing the steps of washing hands and sitting on the mat. Mark *No* if the teacher gives too many directions at once or fails to individualize to the children's level of understanding and children demonstrate confusion or difficulty following through. Score *N/A* if no toddlers are present.

Figure 4.9 illustrates Item 9 Indicators from the TPITOS Scoring Form.

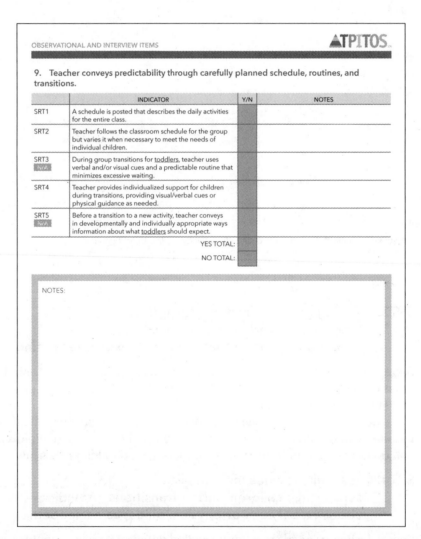

Figure 4.9.   Item 9. Teacher conveys predictability through carefully planned schedule, routines, and transitions (SRT).

Item 10. Environment Is Arranged to Foster Social-Emotional Development (EA)

EA1. Early learning environment includes a variety of developmentally appropriate toys and play areas to support engagement and social interaction.

A variety of toys are available to meet the developmental needs of every child in the classroom. In general, all children engaged in a particular activity should have access to at least the minimum number of items or materials needed for that activity. For example, during block time, there should be adequate numbers of blocks such that all children can engage in that activity. This would apply to, for example, the three children allowed to play in the block "station" but not necessarily all children in the classroom. In another example, while playing ball, each child engaged in this activity should have access to at least one ball. Score *Yes* if toys and/or materials are available, and they are arranged in a way that every child can access toys and materials and that duplicates of favorite toys are made available. At least some age-appropriate materials should be available to promote pretend play. This item may still be scored *Yes* when it is clear that a teacher has intentionally limited the availability of some materials in order to promote child communication or social interactions and materials are ultimately "available" to children. Score *No* if a variety of toys and play areas that can be used in supporting engagement or interaction are not present.

EA2. Play spaces are designed for use by multiple children and to promote social interaction.

Score *Yes* if the environment has defined play areas, some of which are smaller for small groups to engage in play and other areas that are large enough to promote more active play and large motor movement. There should be a variety of spaces available for different types of play (e.g., soft and open spaces for early walkers, soft floor space for infants, themed "stations" or play areas for toddlers). Score *No* if play areas do not have enough toys or materials to accommodate multiple children or do not allow for or promote social interaction.

EA3. In rooms for <u>infants</u> younger than 12 months, there is open space for <u>infants</u> to have "tummy time."

Score *Yes* if there are children younger than 12 months old, and the classroom has protected space away from children who are runners and walkers so that these infants can be safe while they lay on their stomachs. Score *No* if there are children younger than 12 months but there is no protected space. Score *N/A* if there are no infants younger than 12 months.

EA4. In rooms for <u>toddlers </u>who are capable of running, traffic patterns in the classroom are arranged so that there are no wide open spaces for running.

Score *Yes* if the room is arranged in a way that limits the availability of wide open spaces that might encourage older children to run. Score *No* if there are wide open spaces in the classroom. Score *N/A* if no toddlers are present.

EA5. Books, materials, and posters that foster social awareness and help children learn about cultural and individual differences are available.

Score *Yes* if the classroom has materials out and available that show children and families from different cultural backgrounds, that contain pictures of children with

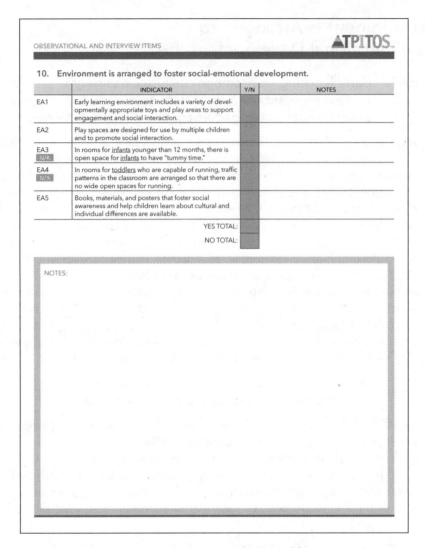

Figure 4.10.   Item 10. Environment is arranged to foster social-emotional development (EA).

and without disabilities, and that show pictures of children with varying emotional expressions. The presence of posted pictures and/or picture books of the children's families who are enrolled in the classroom also need to be observed to score *Yes*.

Figure 4.10 illustrates Item 10 Indicators from the TPITOS Scoring Form.

Item 11. Teacher Collaborates with His or Her Peers (e.g., Other Teachers, Mental Health Practitioners, Allied Health Professionals) to Support Children's Social-Emotional Development (TCP)

TCP1.   Almost all interactions in the classroom between the teacher and his or her peers are related to children or classroom activities.

Score *Yes* if almost all of the exchanges between the focal teacher and other classroom adults (e.g., teacher aides, volunteers) are positive, appropriate, and primarily related to classroom topics (e.g., coordinating changing and feeding schedules for children). Score *No* if you observe multiple or lengthy instances of the teacher talking with other teachers about nonclassroom–related topics, such as weekend activities. Score *N/A* if no other adults are present.

TCP2. All teachers are engaged with children during classroom activities or routines.

Score *Yes* when all teachers are attending to children in some manner throughout the observation (e.g., playing blocks, assisting with transitions). Preparing activities, talking to parents, and/or observing children are classroom duties that may separate children from a teacher but should not be counted against the teacher. Score *No*, when teachers are sitting away from children and talking to each other about weekend activities during outdoor play, for example.

TCP3. The tone of adult voices is positive toward other classroom adults.

Score *Yes* if the teacher's verbal/nonverbal communication toward other adults in the classroom is supportive and positive. The teacher's communications should be a model for children in the classroom (e.g., positive, supportive). Score *No* if the teacher belittles or scolds other classroom adults or is talking negatively about others.

TCP4. The classroom runs smoothly with all adults appearing to know what they are supposed to be doing throughout the observation.

Teachers and classroom staff are coordinated with regard to classroom roles and activities. Score *Yes* if classroom adults understand their role and what comes next in the daily routine. Score *No* if the teacher appears confused as classroom routines and activities change. (Allowances should be made for teachers who are new to the classroom and just learning classroom routines.)

TCP5. Teacher describes ways in which he or she has shared information and communicated with allied health professionals (e.g., PT, OT) (INT).

Score *Yes* if the teacher describes examples of how information is shared and communicated. A teacher may describe how he or she shares successes and challenges with other professionals on a child's team through phone calls, notes, emails, or visits to the classroom. For example, a teacher may report informing the occupational therapist and parents about improvements in a child's fine motor skills or sharing information frequently with allied health professionals. Score *Yes* if the teacher describes how she ensures this communication takes place. Score *No* if the teacher does not describe any examples of having shared information with team members or parents or if the examples were "one-time" instances and not a frequent practice. Although this item refers primarily to communications with allied health professionals, these communications may also include parents. If a teacher reports on communication with parents only and not with professionals, score *No*. Score *N/A* if the teacher has not or does not currently have the opportunity to communicate with other professionals regarding children within the classroom.

TCP6. Teacher reports incorporating information communicated by or with other members of the team and with parents into classroom practices to ensure all needs are met (INT).

A teacher might indicate that he or she uses an AAC device during free play for a nonverbal child, based on the recommendations of a child's speech-language pathologist. A teacher may also report making modifications to a specific routine to prevent challenging behavior for a specific child. Score *Yes* if the teacher demonstrates evidence of incorporating this type of information into classroom practices. Score *No* if the teacher does not describe any examples of incorporating such information into practices or if the teacher does not communicate with team members. The teacher should refer to the information communicated with allied health professionals in order to score this indicator *Yes*. If the teacher reports incorporating communications with parents only and not with professionals, score *No*. Score *N/A* if the teacher has not or does not currently have the opportunity to communicate with other professionals regarding children within the classroom.

Figure 4.11 illustrates Item 11 Indicators from the TPITOS Scoring Form.

Figure 4.11. Item 11. Teacher collaborates with his or her peers (e.g., other teachers, mental health practitioners, allied health professionals) to support children's social-emotional development (TCP).

Item 12. Teacher Has Effective Strategies for Engaging Parents in Supporting Their Children's Social-Emotional Development and Addressing Challenging Behaviors (EEP)

EEP1.   **Teacher describes ways in which families are provided information about social-emotional development (INT).**

Score *Yes* if the teacher reports that he or she shares information with parents about social-emotional development, such as typical milestones in social-emotional development. This might include providing general parenting resources or information specific to the individual child. Score *No* if the examples described are not specific to social-emotional development.

EEP2.   **Teacher describes giving families practical strategies that they can use to promote their children's social-emotional development, prevent challenging behavior, or address other behavioral concerns (INT).**

Score *Yes* if the teacher indicates that he or she shares specific strategies with parents. This might include general strategies provided in a class-wide handout or specific strategies shared with a particular family. Score *No* if the information shared is not specific to social-emotional development or child behavior.

EEP3.   **Teacher indicates that when there is a concern about a child's social-emotional development or challenging behavior he or she works together with parents to collect information on the behavior to determine if there is a need for more intensive support (INT).**

This might involve parent–teacher conferences, phone calls, or emails or implementing a notebook that is sent between home and the center on a regular basis for information sharing. Even if the teacher indicates there are no children present with concerns about social-emotional development or challenging behavior, ask the teacher to report on how he or she would work together with parents. If information sharing and communication are not related to the collection of or sharing of child-specific information, score *No*.

EEP4.   **Teacher describes providing families with information on community resources related to children's social-emotional development (e.g., parenting classes or mental health services) (INT).**

This may involve information sharing through handouts, posted information, newsletters, emails, and so forth. Score *Yes* if the teacher describes examples of information that has been shared with families regarding social-emotional development. Score *No* if the information is not specific to social-emotional development or child behavior.

EEP5.   **When a <u>toddler</u> has significant behavior challenges, teacher indicates that he or she works together with the family and other mental health support services to develop and implement a behavior support plan (INT).**

Once significant behavior challenges and the need for a behavior support plan have been identified, a plan is developed through collaboration with other professionals and/or by

Figure 4.12.   Item 12. Teacher has effective strategies for engaging parents in supporting their child's social-emotional development and addressing challenging behavior (EEP).

working directly with parents. Score *Yes* if the teacher reports that he or she works together with the families (e.g., communication, meetings, coordinating with other professionals) regarding behavior support plans. Score *No* if the teacher does not describe how he or she worked together with families in these situations. Score *N/A* if there are no significant behavior challenges with a behavior support plan or there are no toddlers present.

Figure 4.12 illustrates Item 12 Indicators from the TPITOS Scoring Form.

Item 13. Teacher Has Effective Strategies for Communicating with Families and Promoting Family Involvement in the Classroom (CWF)

CWF1.   Teacher reports that he or she regularly provides families with information on what is going on in the classroom (INT).

Score *Yes* if the teacher reports communicating (e.g., e-mail, bulletin board, mobile apps) with caregivers about regular and special classroom events (e.g., holiday parties, staffing changes) and provides them with ample notice so they can make arrangements to participate, when appropriate. Score *No* if the teacher does not describe any instances of information sharing in regard to classroom activities.

CWF2. Teacher reports a system for communicating with families about the daily experiences of individual children (INT).

Score *Yes* if the teacher indicates that he or she uses methods such as daily reports, e-mails, phone calls, or text messaging to keep caregivers informed of children's daily experiences in the classroom. Score *No* if these communications are infrequent or do not occur.

CWF3. Teacher's responses indicate that he or she has different approaches to reach different families (INT).

Score *Yes* if the teacher describes how he or she has used different modes of communication with different families based on family differences. Score *No* if all modes of communication are the same for all children.

CWF4. Teacher describes a system for getting information from families on an ongoing basis about what is happening at home with children (INT).

Score *Yes* if the teacher describes ways he or she learns about what is happening in the home that may affect children's interactions with peers and classroom adults (e.g., changes in family makeup, job loss, and sleep difficulties). Score *No* if the teacher does not describe strategies for learning about such child-specific information.

CWF5. Teacher describes a variety of strategies for promoting family involvement in the classroom (INT).

Score *Yes* if the teacher indicates a variety of differentiated approaches (e.g., email, newsletter, offering suggestions as to how parents can find time, offering choices) to support caregiver involvement in the classroom on a regular basis (e.g., volunteering in the classroom, visiting the classroom, reading a story to the class, preparing classroom materials, donating supplies). Score *No* if there is only one strategy to promote family involvement or if the opportunities for involvement are limited to just infrequent, special events (e.g., classroom parties).

Figure 4.13 illustrates Item 13 Indicators from the TPITOS Scoring Form.

RED FLAGS

Score Red Flags for individual teachers or entire classroom, as indicated. Red Flag Items 1–3, 5, 6, and 9 are scored for individual teachers, whereas Red Flag Items 4, 7, 10, and 11 are scored for the entire classroom. Red Flag Item 8 can be scored for either the individual teacher being observed or for the classroom. In some cases, you may observe Red Flags being demonstrated by other teachers in the classroom. Because Red Flags indicate a need for more immediate feedback, you may score these items for other teachers in the classroom. When you note the presence of a Red Flag for a teacher who is not the primary one being observed, these scores are not incorporated into the TPITOS score.

At least one example and nonexample are provided for each Red Flag behavior. Note that "nonexamples" are behaviors that do would *not* be scored as Red Flag

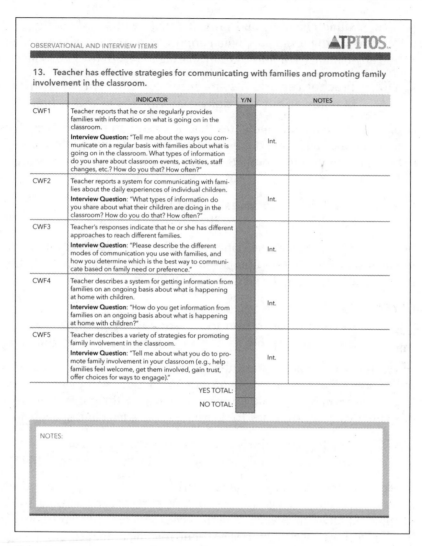

Figure 4.13. Item 13. Teacher has effective strategies for communicating with families and promoting family involvement in the classroom (CWF).

behavior but are also not necessarily considered recommended practice. Figure 4.14 illustrates Red Flags from the TPITOS Scoring Form.

Responsive to Individual Children

1. **Children spend large amounts of time disengaged, without assistance from this teacher to become engaged.**

Examples: Children are left in play area for extended periods of time without teacher engagement; teacher is on his or her cell phone for long periods of time.

Nonexample: Teacher sits on the floor with children, is supportive of children, and is engaged in a finger paint activity but glances at his or her phone briefly.

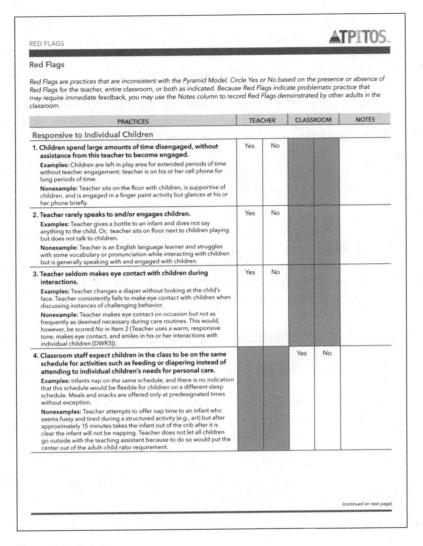

Figure 4.14.   Red Flags.

2.   Teacher rarely speaks to and/or engages children.

Examples: Teacher gives a bottle to an infant and does not say anything to the child. Or, teacher sits on floor next to children playing but does not talk to children.

Nonexample: Teacher is an English-Language Learner and struggles with some vocabulary or pronunciation while interacting with children but is generally speaking with and engaged with children.

3.   Teacher seldom makes eye contact with children during interactions.

Examples: Teacher changes a diaper without looking at the child's face. Teacher consistently fails to make eye contact with children when discussing instances of challenging behavior.

Nonexample: Teacher makes eye contact on occasion but not as frequently as deemed necessary during care routines. This would, however, be scored *No* in Item 2 (Teacher uses a warm, responsive tone, makes eye contact, and smiles in his or her interactions with individual children [DWR3]).

4. **Classroom staff expect children in the class to be on the same schedule for activities such as feeding or diapering instead of attending to individual children's needs for personal care.**

Examples: Infants nap on the same schedule, and there is no indication that this schedule would be flexible for children on a different sleep schedule. Meals and snacks are offered only at predesignated times without exception.

Nonexamples: Teacher attempts to offer nap time to an infant who seems fussy and tired during a structured activity (e.g., art) but after approximately 15 minutes takes the infant out of the crib after it is clear the infant will not be napping. Teacher does not let all children go outside with the teaching assistant because to do so would put the center out of the adult–child ratio requirement.

Promoting Emotional Expression and Social Interaction

5. **Teacher uses flat affect when talking with infants and toddlers.**

Examples: While talking with a child, teacher's tone of voice is flat and lacks any emotion or enthusiasm. Teacher leads activities, such as story-book time and playtime, without any excitement and with flat affect.

Nonexample: Teacher's affect is uncharacteristically flat during a brief play period of the observation, but you observe the teacher to be expressive and animated throughout most of the observation.

6. **Teacher speaks harshly to children.**

Examples: Teacher uses a harsh or negative tone while responding to a child. Teacher uses large amounts of sarcasm when talking with children.

Nonexample: Teacher's tone could be interpreted as "firm" when discussing ongoing biting incidences between a biter and the one bitten. Out of context this could appear harsh, but based on your observation, you see that in general, the tone of the teacher's communication to children is positive. This may, however, be scored as *No* in Item 7 (Teacher's tone remains calm, supportive, and positive during children's distressful or challenging episodes [RDC1]).

Responds to Children's Distress and Challenging Behavior

7. **Children seem generally unhappy or upset.**

Example: Multiple children spend a greater amount of time crying or fussing than might be expected (e.g., more than just the time it takes to finish what the teacher is doing and then responding; 5–10 minutes of not responding), or the majority of the children are unhappy or upset.

Nonexample: Teacher tells children they will not be going outside because of weather conditions, and multiple children become upset until they become engaged in an indoor activity.

8. **Children who are distressed are left unattended.**

Examples: Teacher fails to attend to an infant crying in a crib or infant seat. A child has climbed up the slide and become scared and upset, and the teacher fails to respond in reasonable amount of time.

Nonexample: Teacher is using planned ignoring with a child but is still attempting to redirect the child toward an appropriate activity.

Note: This Red Flag may be scored for either an individual teacher or for the classroom, but not for both.

9. **When problem behaviors occur, teacher uses punitive practices.**

Example: When problem behaviors occur, the teacher responds by ignoring the child, using time-out, asking the parent to take the child home, ridiculing the child, speaking in a harsh tone or yelling, and/or pointing out the child's behavior to other adults or children.

Nonexample: Teacher firmly points out child's behavior as a safety reminder (e.g., "Remember when Pete climbed up on the shelves and they fell over? Feet on the floor please.").

Environmental Support for Social Engagement

10. **The environment is set up such that children are isolated from each other for long periods of time.**

Examples: Infants remain awake in cribs for extended periods of time (e.g., 30 minutes after nap) or in infant seats for lengthy periods of time without the ability to interact with other children. Children spend large amounts of time (20–30 minutes) involved in solitary activities (e.g., playing with playdough alone, playing alone on the computer).

Nonexample: A child who chooses to play alone with a toy is allowed to do so, but shortly thereafter, teacher approaches and follows the child's lead as he or she joins in the activity.

11. **The environment is arranged in a way that prevents children from engaging with materials, toys, and/or activities.**

Examples: Children remain in cribs or infant seats for extended periods of time or materials, toys, or books are primarily stored out of reach of children. A room for infants and young toddlers is arranged in such a way that it is more preschool oriented.

Nonexample: Materials that require teacher supervision are placed out of reach of children (e.g., art or craft materials, shaving cream for sensory exploration).

CHAPTER 5

Scoring the Teaching Pyramid Infant–Toddler Observation Scale and Summarizing Results

Chapters 3 and 4 described the TPITOS administration procedures as well as the Indicator Elaborations and Red Flag scoring guidelines. Once the observation and interview are finished, you will have completed your observation and interview notes and provided a *Yes, No,* or *N/A* score to each Indicator within each routine. The next step is to calculate TPITOS scoring based on the information you have gathered. In this chapter, we describe the procedures for assigning overall Indicator and Item scores. We also describe how the TPITOS Excel Scoring Spreadsheets can be used to provide reports and graphs that summarize TPITOS scores and can be used to inform professional development efforts.

SCORING THE INDICATORS

Once you have completed the observation and the interview, the next step, as described in Chapter 3, is to use your notes and the teacher's interview responses to complete the process of scoring each Indicator with a *Yes* or *No* (or *N/A* when the Elaborations indicate this is permitted) and complete scoring of each of the Red Flags. In completing Indicator scoring, Indicators for Items 1–7 should have been scored for each routine observed. Items 8–13 should have been scored once for the entire observation period. To complete the scoring for each Indicator, and within each routine, review the notes from your observation and information gathered from the interview to determine whether each practice was observed or was reported as being used by the teacher during the interview (for Items that allow interview follow-up to be used for scoring). Review the Elaborations provided in Chapter 4 carefully to be sure the criterion for each Indicator has been met. For Items 1–7, enter a score of *Yes, No,* or *N/A* for each Indicator, within each routine observed. For Items 8–11, enter a score of *Yes, No,* or *N/A* for each Indicator for the observation period. Incorporate responses to the interview questions into your Item scores. For the Red Flags, enter a score of *Yes* or *No* for either the teacher or the classroom, as indicated on the TPITOS Scoring Form. To review, be sure to follow these guidelines in completing your scoring:

- For Items 1–7, provide a score of *Yes, No,* or *N/A* for each Indicator, within each routine observed. Write scores in the appropriate cells.

- For Items 8–13, provide a score of *Yes, No,* or *N/A* for each Indicator for the whole observation period.

- Use *N/A* only when the Elaboration indicates the use of *N/A* is allowed. Refer to the Elaborations, as well as Appendix B, to determine the Indicators for which *N/A* is allowed. Write *N/A* in the appropriate cell.

- When observing in an infant classroom or a mixed-age classroom, refer to the Indicator names to determine whether "toddler" or "infant" is underlined. These Items may be scored as *N/A* if they are not applicable to the age group you are observing. Write *N/A* in the appropriate cell.

- Ask interview questions and use the teacher's response in your scoring only when indicated this is permitted on the TPITOS Scoring Form and when you cannot give a score of *Yes* or *No* based on the observation alone. Indicators for which an interview question is permitted are indicated by *Int.* in the notes column of the TPITOS Scoring Form.

- When you have asked an interview question, use the interview response to score the Indicator by determining whether the practices described by the teacher would lead you to score *Yes* or *No*.

Determining Overall Item Scores

For Items 1–7, once each Indicator under each routine has been scored, the next step is to determine the overall Indicator score. Each Indicator should have a score of *Yes*, *No*, or *N/A* for at least three different routines observed (i.e., free play, structured group, personal care, or outdoors). The overall Indicator score is also a *Yes*, *No*, or *N/A* and is determined by the score given for the greatest number of routines within the Indicator. The score given to the majority of routines within a given Indicator determines the overall Indicator score. For example, if three of the three routines observed were scored *Yes* or if two of the three routines observed were scored *Yes*, then the overall Indicator score is *Yes*. Similarly, if four routines were observed, and three routines were scored *Yes* and one was scored *No*, the overall Indicator score would be *Yes* because that was the score most frequently given. Conversely, if three of three Indicators, or two of the three Indicators were scored *No*, then the overall Indicator score is *No*. Figure 5.1 provides an example of how to score each Indicator within Item 1. For Indicator CBR1, free play, structured group, and personal care practices were scored *Yes*. Because the majority of routines scored (three of three) were scored with a *Yes*, the overall Indicator score is *Yes*. For CBR2, all three routines were scored *No*, so the overall Indicator score is *No*. For CBR3, structured group was scored *Yes*, whereas free play and personal care practices were scored *No*, so the overall Indicator score is *No*. For CBR4, free play and structured group routines were scored *Yes*, whereas personal care practices was scored *No*, so the overall Indicator score is *Yes*. For CBR8, *N/A* was scored for each routine because there were no children who had language delays or were DLLs.

Reconciling an Equal Number of *Yes* and *No* Scores

In cases in which an even number of routines were scored *Yes* or *No*, such as when only two routines were scored and the third was scored with *N/A*, or when two were scored *Yes* and two were scored *No*, the overall Indicator score is determined by taking two factors into consideration and making a decision about whether the overall Indicator score should be *Yes* or *No*. The observer should take into account

1. How much time was spent observing the teacher within each routine? The scores from those routines that were observed for a longer period of time should have

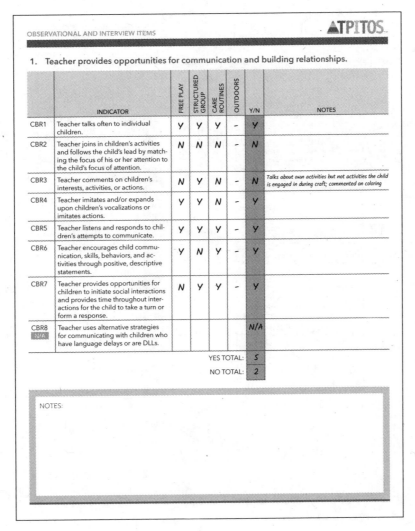

Figure 5.1. Example of Indicator scoring for Item 1. Teacher Provides Opportunities for Communication and Building Relationships.

a higher "weight" in determining the overall score. For example, if the observer spent 45 minutes observing free play, 45 minutes on structured group activities, 15 minutes on care practices, and 15 minutes outdoors, the observer will rely more heavily on the free play and structured group activity scores to determine the overall score.

2. What was the general quality of the practices you observed? When implementation of the practices observed are of a higher quality or fidelity and when they are implemented consistently across the majority of interactions, this would result in a higher overall score. Lower quality and less frequent practices would result in a lower overall score.

Figure 5.2 provides examples for how to score Indicators for which there are an even number of routine scores. For Item 7 (Teacher responds to children in distress and manages challenging behaviors), three routines were observed and scored (free play, structured group, and personal care practices), but because there were no instances of challenging behavior or distress during the brief structured group portion

OBSERVATIONAL AND INTERVIEW ITEMS   ▲TPITOS™

7.   Teacher responds to children in distress and manages challenging behaviors.

	INDICATOR	FREE PLAY	STRUCTURED GROUP	CARE ROUTINES	OUTDOORS	Y/N	NOTES
RDC1 N/A	Teacher's tone remains calm, supportive, and positive during children's distressful or challenging episodes.	Y	n/a	Y	–	Y	
RDC2 N/A	Teacher immediately responds to children in distress to assess children's status.	Y	n/a	Y	–	Y	
RDC3 N/A	Teacher provides positive attention to toddlers when they have calmed down and are behaving appropriately.	N	n/a	Y	–	N	Gave child a toy two times during free play when crying and stomping; missed several opportunities to give positive attention; gave child more snack one time once child calmed and requested
RDC4 N/A	Teacher uses a challenging situation as an opportunity to help children recognize and deal with emotions.	N	n/a	N	–	N	Told child to calm down; did not reflect feelings
RDC5 N/A	Teacher provides support to toddlers who are angry or upset to help them with problem solving, when appropriate.	Y	n/a	N	–	Y	Helped problem-solve many times during free play; used multiple techniques to teach how to handle situations and talked about related emotions (e.g., frustrated, sad); same skills were not utilized during snack
RDC6 N/A	Teacher uses strategies such as redirection and/or planned ignoring with individual toddlers who are in distress or engage in occasional episodes of challenging behavior. **Interview Question:** "Tell me what strategies you follow when children have occasional episodes of challenging behavior (e.g., physical aggression, screaming, taking others' toys)?"	Y	n/a	Y	–	Y	Obs. Int.
RDC7 N/A	Teacher uses a variety of strategies to console, soothe, or calm children who are in distress and individualizes responses according to children and situations. **Interview Question:** "Tell me about different ways that you comfort children who are in distress (e.g., picking up an infant, problem solving with a toddler)?"	Y	n/a	Y	–	Y	When children are sad at drop off, gives hugs and helps them find a friend in the room Obs. Int.
					YES TOTAL:	5	
					NO TOTAL:	2	

NOTES:

Figure 5.2.   Example of Indicator scoring for Teacher Responds to Children in Distress and Manages Challenging Behaviors.

of the observation, these Indicators were not scored and *N/A* was entered. For RDC1 in Item 7, both free play and personal care practices were scored *Yes*, so the overall Indicator is *Yes*. Similarly, for RDC4, both free play and personal care practices were scored *No*, so the overall Indicator is *No*.

For RDC3, personal care was scored *Yes*, but a *No* was scored during free play. In this case, the observer takes the two criteria described previously into account to determine the overall Indicator score. The observer determines the overall score by considering how much time was spent observing each routine and the general quality of the observed practices. In this scenario, the observation took place during a total of 1 hour of free play time, 20 minutes of care routines, and about 40 minutes of structured group activities. Because there were no instances of challenging behavior or distress during structured group activity, the overall score for RDC Indicators is based on 1 hour of free play and 20 minutes of care practices. For RDC3, the practice was observed and scored *No* during free play and *Yes* during care practices. The observation notes indicate that the teacher missed opportunities to engage in this practice on multiple occasions during free play but did engage in this practice once during a care practice. Thus, free play, observed over 1 hour, yielded a *No*, whereas care routines, observed over 20 minutes, yielded a *Yes*. Furthermore, there are multiple incidents in which the practice was "missed" during free play, while there was only one instance of the practice during a care practice. Thus, the overall Indicator score is a *No* for RDC3. Greater weight was placed on the score for free play in determining the overall Indicator score because the teacher was observed in free play for a longer period of time, and the teacher missed multiple opportunities to engage in this practice in free play, compared with demonstrating the practice only once during care practices.

In another example in Figure 5.2, RDC5, a *Yes* was scored during free play, although a *No* was scored during personal care practices. The notes indicate that again, there were multiple opportunities for this practice, helping children problem-solve during challenging situations and during free play. Furthermore, the notes indicate that the teacher was highly skilled in this practice. The teacher helped children understand emotions and helped them understand different ways to handle the situation. During care practices, however, the teacher did not engage in this way. Therefore, for RDC5, the overall Indicator score is determined to a greater degree by the *Yes* provided for free play. The teacher used the practices and met the criteria outlined in the Elaboration for 1 hour of the 2-hour period. The observer noted that the quality of the practice was high, and the teacher was observed to use those practices multiple times during free play. Observers must take these criteria into account when assigning an overall Indicator score when there is a "tie" in the scores given to an Indicator across routines and take all evidence of use or the lack of use of these practice into account to provide the overall Indicator score.

Items Given One Score for 2-Hour Observation

As you complete the overall Indicator scores, note that for Items 8–11, scores are based on the overall observation period and *not* within specific routines. Thus, you will score those Items with *Yes* or *No* based on the entire 2-hour observation period. These are Items that reflect practices that are not related to specific routines or are implemented across routines, such as Item 8, which pertains to strategies or modifications for children with disabilities or delays; Item 10, which addresses the physical environment; or Item 11, on how teachers work together in the classroom. Items 12 and 13 represent practices that are not likely to be observed during a classroom observation and are scored solely on the teacher's responses to interview Items. These Items pertain to how teachers communicate with and engage parents. Figure 5.3 provides an example of scoring for Item 12 (Teacher has effective strategies for engaging parents in supporting their children's social-emotional development and addressing challenging behaviors). Indicators under Item 12 are scored based on teacher responses to interview questions and not based on the observation, so they are also only scored once and not across routines.

Completing Indicator Scoring

Review the TPITOS Scoring Form to ensure that there is an overall Indicator score for each Indicator. Upon completing the scoring process for observation and interview Items, there should be a *Yes*, *No*, or *N/A* score for each Indicator, entered into the shaded overall Indicator score column. Once all of the Indicators are scored, sum

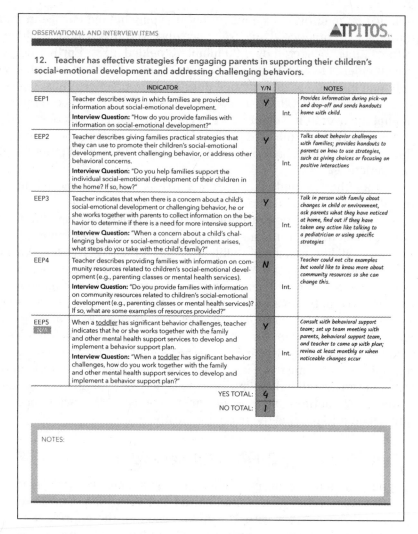

OBSERVATIONAL AND INTERVIEW ITEMS   ▲TPITOS™

12.   Teacher has effective strategies for engaging parents in supporting their children's social-emotional development and addressing challenging behaviors.

	INDICATOR	Y/N	NOTES
EEP1	Teacher describes ways in which families are provided information about social-emotional development. **Interview Question:** "How do you provide families with information on social-emotional development?"	Y Int.	*Provides information during pick-up and drop-off and sends handouts home with child.*
EEP2	Teacher describes giving families practical strategies that they can use to promote their children's social-emotional development, prevent challenging behavior, or address other behavioral concerns. **Interview Question:** "Do you help families support the individual social-emotional development of their children in the home? If so, how?"	Y Int.	*Talks about behavior challenges with families; provides handouts to parents on how to use strategies, such as giving choices or focusing on positive interactions*
EEP3	Teacher indicates that when there is a concern about a child's social-emotional development or challenging behavior, he or she works together with parents to collect information on the behavior to determine if there is a need for more intensive support. **Interview Question:** "When a concern about a child's challenging behavior or social-emotional development arises, what steps do you take with the child's family?"	Y Int.	*Talk in person with family about changes in child or environment, ask parents what they have noticed at home, find out if they have taken any action like talking to a pediatrician or using specific strategies*
EEP4	Teacher describes providing families with information on community resources related to children's social-emotional development (e.g., parenting classes or mental health services). **Interview Question:** "Do you provide families with information on community resources related to children's social-emotional development (e.g., parenting classes or mental health services)? If so, what are some examples of resources provided?"	N Int.	*Teacher could not cite examples but would like to know more about community resources so she can change this.*
EEP5 N/A	When a toddler has significant behavior challenges, teacher indicates that he or she works together with the family and other mental health support services to develop and implement a behavior support plan. **Interview Question:** "When a toddler has significant behavior challenges, how do you work together with the family and other mental health support services to develop and implement a behavior support plan?"	Y Int.	*Consult with behavioral support team; set up team meeting with parents, behavioral support team, and teacher to come up with plan; review at least monthly or when noticeable changes occur*

YES TOTAL: 4

NO TOTAL: 1

NOTES:

Figure 5.3.   Example of Indicator scoring for Teacher has Effective Strategies for Engaging Parents in Supporting Their Children's Social-Emotional Development and Addressing Challenging Behaviors.

the number of *Yes* scores and the number of *No* scores at the bottom of each Item table. Figure 5.4 shows an example of the sum of *Yes* scores and the sum of *No* scores for Item 4. Four of the five Indicators were scored *Yes*, so "4" is filled in as the sum of *Yes* scores and "1" is filled in for the sum of *No* scores. Be sure to review the score sheet to ensure the process has been completed for each Item before moving on to the Red Flags.

SCORING THE RED FLAGS

After scoring all of the Observational and Interview Items, the next step is to complete Red Flag scoring. There are 11 Red Flags, and each is scored by circling *Yes* or *No*. Red Flags 1–3, 5, 6, and 9 pertain to the observed teacher. Red Flags 4, 7, 10, and 11 pertain to the whole classroom. Red Flag 8 can be scored for either the observed teacher or the whole classroom but is scored only once. Figures 5.5–5.7 show examples of Red Flag scoring for one observation. Three Red Flags were scored *Yes* for the observed teacher.

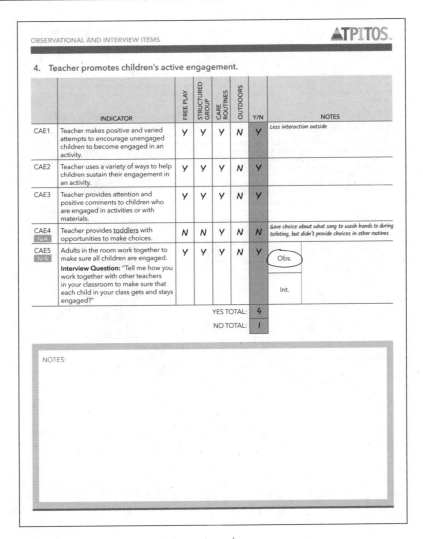

Figure 5.4. Example of Item scoring.

Two Red Flags were scored for the classroom, including Red Flag 8. Because Red Flag 8 was scored for the classroom, it should not also be scored for the individual teacher. There is a total of five *Yes* scores for the Red Flags during this observation.

SUMMARIZING TPITOS ITEM SCORES

After all of the Indicators have an overall Indicator score and all of the Red Flags are scored, the next step is to determine the percentage score for each Item score. The Item score is the percentage of Indicators scored with a *Yes*. There are two methods of summarizing these scores. The first is simply by using the TPITOS Scoring Summary Profile in the TPITOS Scoring Form. The second method is to enter the data into a TPITOS Excel Scoring Spreadsheet.

The TPITOS Scoring Summary Profile in the TPITOS Scoring Form is organized so that the Item score can be calculated from the Indicator scores. For each Item, determine the number of Indicators scored with a *Yes*, and enter the sum in column A (number of Indicators scored *Yes*). Then, determine the total number of Indicators

RED FLAGS **TPITOS**™

Red Flags

Red Flags are practices that are inconsistent with the Pyramid Model. Circle Yes or No based on the presence or absence of Red Flags for the teacher, entire classroom, or both as indicated. Because Red Flags indicate problematic practice that may require immediate feedback, you may use the Notes column to record Red Flags demonstrated by other adults in the classroom.

PRACTICES	TEACHER		CLASSROOM		NOTES
Responsive to Individual Children					
1. Children spend large amounts of time disengaged, without assistance from this teacher to become engaged. **Examples:** Children are left in play area for extended periods of time without teacher engagement; teacher is on his or her cell phone for long periods of time. **Nonexample:** Teacher sits on the floor with children, is supportive of children, and is engaged in a finger paint activity but glances at his or her phone briefly.	Yes	No X			
2. Teacher rarely speaks to and/or engages children. **Examples:** Teacher gives a bottle to an infant and does not say anything to the child. Or, teacher sits on floor next to children playing but does not talk to children. **Nonexample:** Teacher is an English language learner and struggles with some vocabulary or pronunciation while interacting with children but is generally speaking with and engaged with children.	Yes X	No			*Long periods of time with no positive teacher–child interaction*
3. Teacher seldom makes eye contact with children during interactions. **Examples:** Teacher changes a diaper without looking at the child's face. Teacher consistently fails to make eye contact with children when discussing instances of challenging behavior. **Nonexample:** Teacher makes eye contact on occasion but not as frequently as deemed necessary during care routines. This would, however, be scored *No* in Item 2 (Teacher uses a warm, responsive tone, makes eye contact, and smiles in his or her interactions with individual children [DWR3]).	Yes	No X			
4. Classroom staff expect children in the class to be on the same schedule for activities such as feeding or diapering instead of attending to individual children's needs for personal care. **Examples:** Infants nap on the same schedule, and there is no indication that this schedule would be flexible for children on a different sleep schedule. Meals and snacks are offered only at predesignated times without exception. **Nonexamples:** Teacher attempts to offer nap time to an infant who seems fussy and tired during a structured activity (e.g., art) but after approximately 15 minutes takes the infant out of the crib after it is clear the infant will not be napping. Teacher does not let all children go outside with the teaching assistant because to do so would put the center out of the adult-child ratio requirement.			Yes	No X	

(continued on next page)

Figure 5.5. Example of Red Flag scoring.

scored with a *No* and enter that sum in column B (number of Indicators scored *No*). In doing so, count only the *Yes* and the *No* scores. Do not include *N/A* scores in column A or B. In column C, enter the sum of the number of *Yes* scores and the number of *No* scores (A + B). Then, divide the sum of *Yes* scores (column A) by the number of Indicators scored (column C), and multiply by 100 to obtain the percentage of Indicators scored *Yes*. Enter this percentage in column D. This percentage is the Item score; the percentage of Indicators scored *Yes*.

Figure 5.8 provides an example of how to complete the TPITOS Scoring Summary Profile. For example, for Item 3 (Teacher promotes positive peer interactions), six Indicators were scored *Yes* (column A) and two Indicators were scored *No* (column B). The sum of columns A and B (8) is entered in column C, and this is then used to calculate the percentage of Indicators within that Item that were scored *Yes*. (6/[6 + 2] = .75, and .75 × 100 = 75%). Complete these steps for every TPITOS Item to determine the overall Item score for each Item.

To obtain the overall percentage of Indicators scored *Yes*, calculate the sum of the numbers in columns A, B, and C and enter the sum in the shaded "Total" row at the bottom of the table. Divide the column A total by the column C total to obtain the

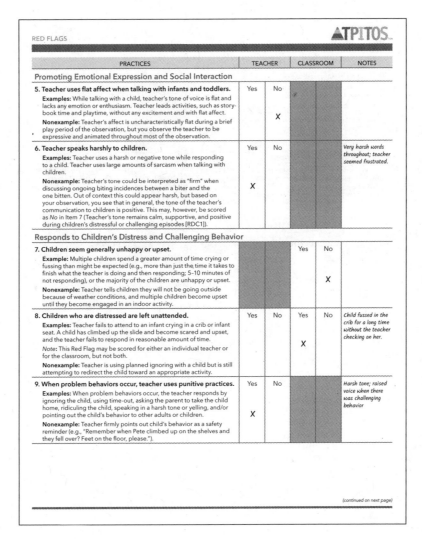

Figure 5.6. Example of Red Flag scoring.

overall percentage of Indicators scored *Yes*. Figure 5.8 provides an example of how to obtain the overall TPITOS percentage score. In column A, there are 43 *Yes* Indicators. In column B, there are 33 *No* Indicators. The sum of columns A and B, 76, is entered in column C. The percentage of all Indicators scored *Yes* is then 57% (43/[43 + 33] = .57, and .57 × 100 = 57%).

This TPITOS Scoring Summary Profile can be used to quickly calculate Item and total TPITOS scores, but it can also be used to summarize data that will then be entered into the TPITOS Excel Scoring Spreadsheet. The contents of columns A and B, which are the total number of *Yes* scores and the total number of *No* scores for each Item, are needed to use the spreadsheet file. The spreadsheet will then calculate the percentage score for each Item, as well as the overall TPITOS score for each observation.

SUMMARIZING RED FLAG SCORES

Red Flags are summarized as the percentage of Red Flags scored *Yes*. Fill in the number of Red Flags scored *Yes* for the observed teacher and for the classroom in column A

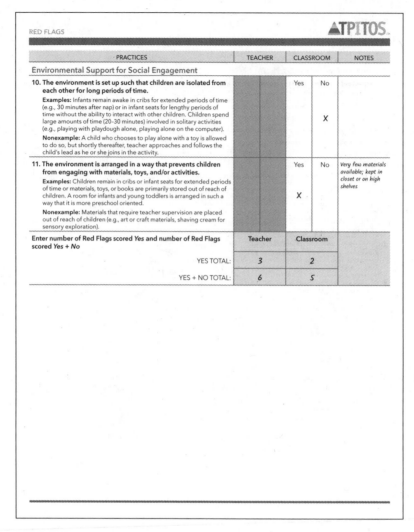

Figure 5.7. Example of Red Flag scoring.

in the Red Flag Scoring Summary. There are a total number of 11 possible Red Flags. Calculate the percentage of Red Flags scored *Yes* by dividing the number of *Yes* Red Flags by 11, the total possible. Regardless of whether Red Flag number 8 is scored for the teacher or the classroom, the total number of Red Flags scored should still be 11. Figure 5.9 provides an example in which there were three Red Flags for the observed teacher, out of six possible Items, and two Red Flags for the classroom, out of five possible Items. Thus, there were a total of five Red Flags for this observation. To obtain the Red Flag subscale percentage score, divide 5 Red Flags scored *Yes* by the total number of Red Flags (11) and multiply the result by 100 (5/11 = .45, and then .45 × 100 = 45%).

USING THE TPITOS EXCEL SCORING SPREADSHEETS

The TPITOS Excel Scoring Spreadsheets can be used to summarize and graph TPITOS data. To support the use of these resources, instructions and a demonstration video are also provided. The data summary file, available for PC and for Mac, allows users

SCORING SUMMARY PROFILE

TPITOS™

Date of observation: ______________________ Start time: ______________________

Program/Center name: ______________________ End time: ______________________

Classroom name: ______________________

Observer name/ID: ______________________ Teacher name/ID: ______________________

OBSERVATIONAL/INTERVIEW ITEMS SCORING SUMMARY

Directions:

Observational/Interview Items 1-13

1. For each Item, record the number of Indicators scored *Yes*. Enter the sum into the appropriate cells in column A. *Exclude* Indicators scored as *N/A*.
2. For each Item, record the number of Indicators scored *No*. Enter the sum into the appropriate cells in column B. *Exclude* Indicators scored as *N/A*.
3. Add the Totals for column A and column B. Enter the sum into the appropriate cells in column C.
4. To obtain the *percentage* of indicators scored *Yes*, divide the Total in column A by the Total in column C and enter the percentage score in the appropriate cells in column D.
5. Use this summary to enter your data into a TPITOS Excel Scoring Spreadsheet available at http://www.brookespublishing.com/tpitos-scoring-spreadsheet.

Observational Items	A. Total number of Indicators scored *Yes*	B. Total number of Indicators scored *No*	C. Total number of Indicators scored. (A + B)	D. Percentage of Indicators scored *Yes* (A / C * 100)
SAMPLE	5	2	7	71%
1 (CBR). Teacher provides opportunities for communication and building relationships.	4	3	7	57%
2 (DWR). Teacher demonstrates warmth and responsivity to individual children.	5	2	7	71%
3 (PPI). Teacher promotes positive peer interactions.	6	2	8	75%
4 (CAE). Teacher promotes children's active engagement.	2	3	5	40%
5 (REF). Teacher is responsive to children's expression of emotions and teaches about feelings.	3	4	7	43%
6 (CBE). Teacher communicates and provides feedback about developmentally appropriate behavioral expectations.	2	5	7	29%
7 (RDC). Teacher responds to children in distress and manages challenging behaviors.	6	1	7	86%
8 (SMD). Teacher uses specific strategies or modifications for children with disabilities/delays or who are DLLs.	2	0	2	100%
9 (SRT). Teacher conveys predictability through carefully planned schedule, routines, and transitions.	2	3	5	40%
10 (EA). Environment is arranged to foster social-emotional development.	4	1	5	80%
11 (TCP). Teacher collaborates with his or her peers (e.g., other teachers, mental health practitioners, allied health professionals) to support children's social-emotional development.	4	2	6	67%
12 (EEP). Teacher has effective strategies for engaging parents in supporting their children's social-emotional development and addressing challenging behaviors.	1	4	5	20%
13 (CWF). Teacher has effective strategies for communicating with families and promoting family involvement in the classroom.	2	3	5	40%
TOTALS:	43	33	76	57%

Figure 5.8. TPITOS Scoring Summary used to summarize TPITOS scores by hand.

to record up to three administrations of a TPITOS for up to 10 teachers. For each teacher, a graphic summary of each TPITOS administration is generated. When multiple observations are entered, the graphs can be used to show change over time. The spreadsheet also allows users to graph multiple teachers' data on one graph. For instance, TPITOS data for three teachers within one infant classroom can be summarized in the one graph to offer a snapshot of classroom practices across teachers. Users can also graph multiple teacher data over time, such as what might be used at the beginning and end of a school year to present teaching team data over time. Users can select different combinations of observation time points, or "waves," and different combinations of teachers to create individualized graphs that can serve the dual purpose of looking at one or more teachers at one or more points in time.

The spreadsheet is organized on tabs within the file, and the first tab, "Instructions," provides directions for how to enter observation data (see Figure 5.10 for the instructions tab). Each teacher's data are entered on his or her own tab (i.e., Teacher 1, Teacher 2, Teacher 3). There are tabs for up to 10 teachers. On each teacher tab, enter

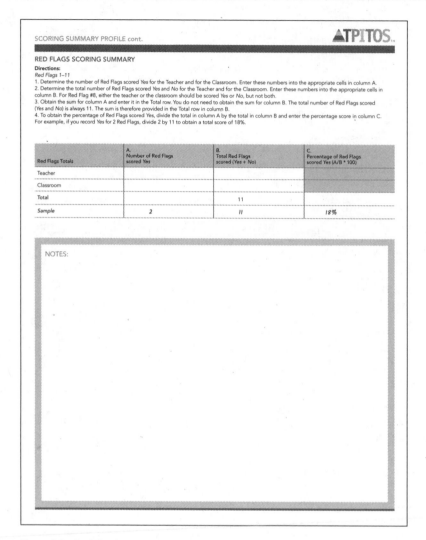

Figure 5.9. Red Flag Scoring Summary.

the teacher and classroom identifier, as well as the program name in the gray boxes at the top of the page. Then, enter the TPITOS observation date where indicated. Up to three observations can be entered per teacher (i.e., Wave 1, Wave 2, Wave 3). For each observation, enter the number of *Yes* scores and the number of *No* scores (again, excluding any *N/A* scores in the counts). The spreadsheet will calculate the percentage of Indicators scored *Yes*, as well as the overall TPITOS score.

For the Red Flags, enter the number of *Yes* Red Flags and the total number of Red Flags possible for the observed teacher and the classroom. The percentage of Red Flags scored *Yes* will be calculated automatically out of 11 possible Red Flags.

After entering the observation and Red Flag data on each teacher tab, the individual teacher graphs are automatically generated (see Figures 5.11 and 5.12). These graphs provide visual summaries of individual teachers over three observation points, which can then be used to provide teacher feedback and inform coaching and professional development efforts.

Additional tabs within the file allow you to view the graphed data of multiple teachers at one, two, or three time points (or waves). Users can select different

Instructions (callouts):

1. Enter the Teacher and Classroom ID (ex: Jane-Class 1) and Program name/ID

2. Enter the date of the TPITOS

3. Enter the number of YES and NO responses for each Item. If you add the numbers, it should equal the number of Indicators for that Item unless there is an option to score N/A. If the score is N/A for an Indicator, do not count it as a YES or NO response. *If a TPITOS is not administered, do not enter any data into the columns. Do not enter "0".

4. Enter the number of YES responses for Red Flags and total # of possible Red Flags for the teacher and the classroom. The sum should always be 11.

Teacher and Classroom name/ID:

Program name/ID:

Observational and Interview Items

TPITOS Item	TPITOS 1 Date: Wave 1			TPITOS 2 Date: Wave 2			TPITOS 3 Date: Wave 3		
	# yes	# no	%	# yes	# no	%	# yes	# no	%
1 Provides opportunities for communication and building relationships									
2 Demonstrates warmth and responsivity to individual children									
3 Promotes positive peer interactions									
4 Promotes children's active engagement									
5 Responsive to children's expression of emotions and teaches about feelings									
6 Communicates and provides feedback about developmentally appropriate behavioral expectations									
7 Responds to children in distress and manages challenging behaviors									
8 Uses specific strategies or modifications for children with disabilities/delays or who are dual language learners									
9 Conveys predictability through carefully planned schedule, routines, and transitions									
10 Environment is arranged to foster social-emotional development									
11 Collaborates with his or her peers to support children's social-emotional development									
12 Has effective strategies for engaging parents in supporting their child's social-emotional development and addressing challenging behaviors									
13 Has effective strategies for communicating with families and promoting family involvement in the classroom									
Average of Items	0	0		0	0		0	0	

Red Flags

Red Flags	# yes	# possible	%	# yes	# possible	%	# yes	# possible	%
Teacher									
Classroom									

Figure 5.10. Instructions for entering data into a TPITOS Excel Scoring Spreadsheet.

73

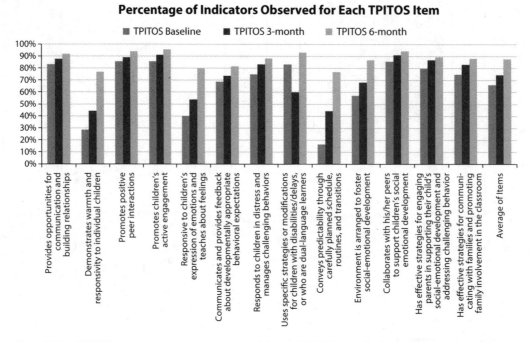

Figure 5.11. TPITOS Item percentage summary scores and the overall TPITOS score for three observations with an individual teacher.

combinations of teachers and waves to display on the graph. For instance, Figure 5.13 shows a graph representing data collected at one point in time from a teaching team of three teachers in one classroom.

Finally, a global summary tab provides graphs that include aggregate data for all teachers entered into the spreadsheet (see Figure 5.14). These graphs can be used for informing classroom- or center-wide professional development efforts.

A second TPITOS Excel Scoring Spreadsheet has a capacity for 40 teachers over three points in time and is also available for PC and for Mac. This resource provides users with the same functionality and may be more appropriate for larger

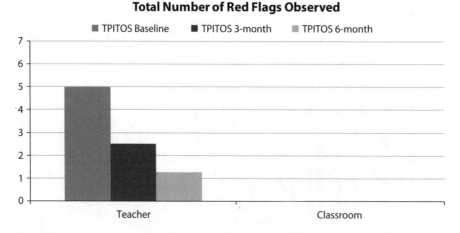

Figure 5.12. Red Flag graph for three observations with an individual teacher.

Percentage of Indicators Observed for Each TPITOS Item

■ Teacher A - Wave 1   ■ Teacher B - Wave 1   ▨ Teacher C - Wave 1

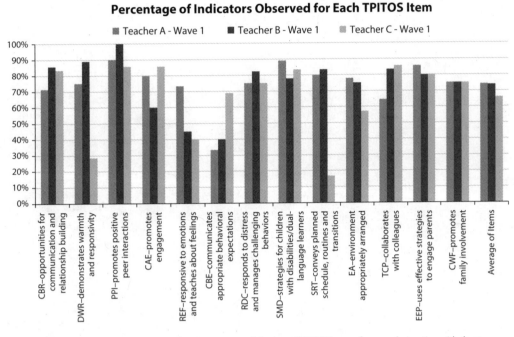

Figure 5.13. TPITOS Item percentage summary scores and the overall TPITOS score for one observation with three different teachers.

program-evaluation efforts or for planning program-wide professional development efforts. For working with individual classrooms, the 10-Teacher capacity spreadsheet is recommended.

These spreadsheets were designed to be flexible and meet the needs of individual classrooms and smaller programs, as well as larger programs. When there is a need to maintain graphs for larger programs with multiple infant or toddler classrooms or multisite programs, it may be helpful to maintain multiple copies of the spreadsheet for use across multiple classrooms.

Program Item Averages

■ Wave 1   ■ Wave 2   ▨ Wave 3

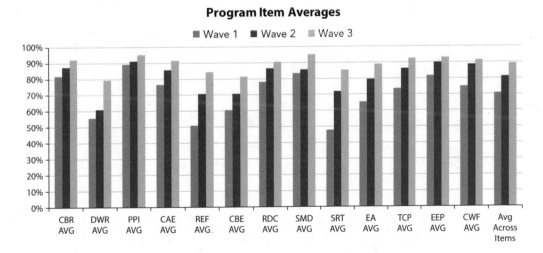

Figure 5.14. Program Item Averages for TPITOS Items and the overall TPITOS scores for one center.

CHAPTER 6

Using the Teaching Pyramid Infant–Toddler Observation Scale to Support Implementation of Effective Practices

Case Studies

The TPITOS can be used in multiple ways, but a primary purpose is to inform professional development efforts. One element of a professional development plan is coaching to support teachers' high-fidelity implementation of teaching and instructional practices such as those measured by the TPITOS. Practice-based coaching is one approach to coaching that has promising evidence (National Center on Quality Teaching and Learning, 2013; Schnitz, Hardy, Artman, & Hemmeter, 2013; Snyder, Hemmeter, & Fox, 2015). Practice-based coaching is implemented in the context of a collaborative partnership between the coach and the teacher and involves goal setting and action planning, focused observations, and reflection and performance feedback. One key component of practice-based coaching is the use of an assessment tool that identifies areas of strengths and needs related to a specific set of practices. The data from such an assessment can be used to identify and set goals for coaching and inform action planning. It can also be used to monitor progress toward goals and evaluate the impact of coaching and professional development on teachers' implementation of *Pyramid Model* practices.

In this chapter, we present two case studies that describe how the TPITOS can be used in the planning, implementation, and evaluation of professional development efforts related to Infant–Toddler Pyramid Model practices. In the first case study, we describe the use of the TPITOS and related professional development efforts conducted with one individual teacher. In the second case study, we describe how the TPITOS can be used in the planning and implementation of programwide professional development efforts.

CASE STUDY 1: USING THE TPITOS TO PROVIDE IMPLEMENTATION SUPPORT TO A TEACHER THROUGH COACHING-BASED PROFESSIONAL DEVELOPMENT

Jason, the lead teacher in a community-based child care center, has been an early educator for 2 years, predominately in preschool classrooms, and has a Child Development

Associate credential. He is currently in pursuit of his bachelor's degree in early childhood education. Jason's classroom includes eight children from 12 to 30 months of age. Of these children, one child is a DLL, one child has Down syndrome, and two children are living in extreme poverty. He had recently begun observing a pattern of challenges in his classroom but struggled to identify the best way to address these issues. He realized that many of the strategies and approaches he learned as a preschool teacher were not necessarily applicable with infants and toddlers. He has a full-time co-teacher, and a Part C early interventionist provides support and guidance in working with the children at risk for or with disabilities roughly 5 hours a week. Over the past year, there have been changes related to supporting infant and toddler social-emotional development via the state's quality rating and improvement system. Jason feels he has a strong team in place for addressing the new guidelines, but he still has some concerns about being able to adhere to the new guidelines and incorporate new practices focusing on social-emotional development for infants and toddlers.

Jason learned about the *Pyramid Model* when he went to a national early childhood conference. He was excited about using the practices to promote children's social-emotional competence. After returning from the conference, he attempted to implement some of the practices to support children's positive relations with peers and their ability to understand their feelings; however, because he was not sure about how to effectively use the practices, he was never able to make the practices stick. The following year, Sarah, his classroom's new mental health consultant, informed him she was now a certified TPITOS observer. She suggested that she conduct TPITOS observations in his classroom and use the TPITOS data to provide him with coaching on infant–toddler social-emotional practices. Jason, remembering his initial excitement about the promise of the *Pyramid Model*, said he would really like to participate. Although very interested in the support, Jason was somewhat nervous about having Sarah come to his classroom observing and potentially judging his ability to use these practices. Upon attending an overview meeting about the coaching model with other providers in the county and learning about how Sarah would be implementing the coaching model, his apprehension soon dissipated. He learned she would not be in an evaluative position, that they would work on developing a collaborative partnership, and that the coaching process would be based on his strengths and needs and the goals for change that he identified with Sarah's assistance.

The initial activities that occurred after his enrollment in the TPITOS professional development program were to meet with Sarah and sign a coaching agreement that included details about the coach–teacher collaborative process. Jason liked that Sarah was enthusiastic about his classroom and the children. Additionally, Sarah's display of empathy when he told her about some of the difficulties he was encountering in the classroom made him feel "heard" and validated his concerns. Upon signing, Jason and Sarah identified a good day to do the initial TPITOS observation. Jason's first meeting with Sarah included an overview of the *Pyramid Model* as well as information that would allow him to reflect on and self-assess his needs and goals related to supporting young children's social-emotional development. Jason indicated he needed some guidance on how to help toddlers better understand the behavioral expectations of the classroom as well as to promote children's active engagement. Excited to begin, he felt that using effective practices in these areas would reduce both behavioral challenges and the frequency with which children in his classroom were in distress.

Sarah administered the TPITOS for her first observation in Jason's classroom later that week in the afternoon. Before starting the observation, Sarah 1) asked Jason what activities would occur during the approximately 2-hour observation and the approximate sequence of when they would occur, 2) explained that she was interested in observing typical routines and interactions during the observation, 3) asked Jason if he could spend about 20 minutes talking with her after the observation, and 4) completed the TPITOS coversheet (e.g., teacher name or identification code, number of DLLs). Sarah then went on to complete the observation, completed the interview with Jason after the children had left for the day, and then scored the TPITOS. Overall, Jason had 66% of all Indicators scored *Yes* and had one Red Flag (Teacher uses flat affect when talking with infants and toddlers). Jason's initial TPITOS scores are displayed in Figure 6.1.

Sarah used these results, along with the results of Jason's self-assessment, to assess Jason's goals as well as identify areas she felt warranted attention. She scheduled a convenient time to meet with Jason and discuss these results. Sarah first began with Jason's strengths, namely 1) being responsive to children's expression of emotions and teaching about feelings, 2) being responsive to children in distress and managing challenging behaviors, and 3) having effective strategies for engaging parents in supporting their children's social-emotional development and addressing challenging behavior. In this first TPITOS observation, Sarah noted that Jason missed several opportunities to demonstrate warmth and responsivity to individual children and to convey predictability through a carefully planned schedule and effective transitions.

A few days after this initial conversation, Sarah and Jason sat down again to finalize goals for an action plan. With Jason's self-assessment and Sarah's TPITOS data,

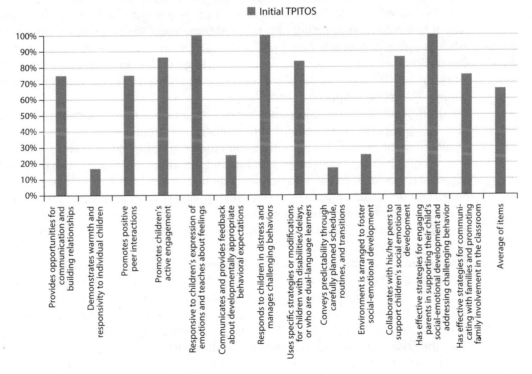

Figure 6.1. Jason's initial TPITOS Indicator scores.

both outlined and agreed on the goals. Using data from the TPITOS observation, Sarah mentioned to Jason that he was particularly warm during one-to-one activities (e.g., book reading, washing hands) but appeared to distance himself from children by always standing while they were on the floor. Sarah also mentioned children transitioned well from hand washing to snack but spent a long time waiting in the entryway on their way to outdoor play, which contributed to some children having difficulty keeping their hands to themselves. Upon bringing this to Jason's attention, he indicated he typically stands because he does not want to interrupt children's play with peers and that he had been told by colleagues he needs to show more affection toward children but is just not a very "touchy-feely" kind of guy. Sarah asked Jason if he had any ideas on how they could work together to take the warmth he displayed in those one-to-one scenarios and transfer it to small group settings as well as create some smoother transitions for children. Jason was not sure about how to increase his warmth toward children but thought that using a transition song and providing visuals might help prepare children for the next activity. Sarah conveyed to him she thought his transition strategies would really help reduce unwanted incidents of challenging behavior, even though he was quite skilled at handling these when they occurred. Understanding his concern about interrupting children's peer play, she suggested spending some short intervals of time on the floor with children and to try offering them some play suggestions based on their interests. After a few successful sessions, she then encouraged Jason to make a conscious attempt to provide some additional eye contact and smiles while providing the play suggestions. This way, there are fewer missed opportunities to show warmth and responsivity toward more children. Furthermore, Sarah thought being on the floor with toddlers and playing an active role in supporting and watching their play skills develop will likely create scenarios where it will be difficult for him to contain his enthusiasm and excitement. Sarah said she understood his concern about disrupting children's interactions with peers but pointed out that teachers play a key role in supporting children's interactions, and that the right amount of adult support at this age helps children develop meaningful friendships. In these discussions, Jason described one additional goal that he had been interested in working on with some of the older toddlers, which was to help children understand behavioral expectations.

Following their reflection and discussion, Jason and Sarah finalized the action plan and prioritized three goals: 1) demonstrating greater warmth toward children, 2) planning for and having smoother transitions in response to Jason's interests and priorities, 3) helping children understand behavioral expectations. The plan included action steps related to each goal, materials that could help him achieve these goals, a timeline for implementing each action step, and information that would allow him to determine when each goal was met. Over the course of 6 months, Jason worked with Sarah, attended additional workshops, and used the CSEFEL videos to provide examples of Pyramid Strategies in infant–toddler settings. Sarah came to his classroom monthly to observe his implementation of practices to find what was working and what was not and to adjust the action plan. Jason often told Sarah how much he liked the debriefing sessions that followed each observation because it brought to light how his use of strategies was improving, and it made him feel more successful as a teacher. Additionally, he said that accomplishing goals and developing new ones kept the coaching sessions relevant, particularly with the number of children moving in and out of his classroom. It also made learning and implementing the strategies seem "do-able." Sarah frequently updated the TPITOS Excel Scoring Spreadsheet

Percentage of Indicators Observed for Each TPITOS Item

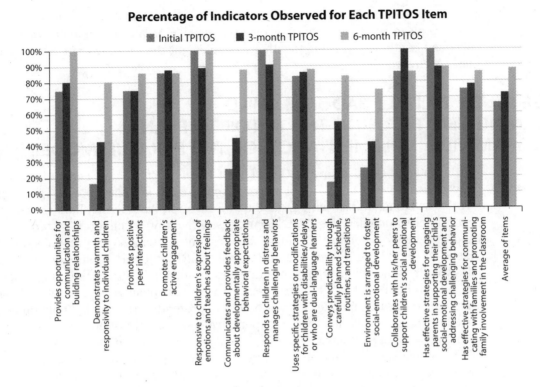

Figure 6.2.   Jason's 6-month TPITOS Indicator scores.

with data from her classroom TPITOS observations, and upon her presenting data based on the 6-month observation, Jason could clearly see growth in the areas their action plan addressed (e.g., greater warmth, smoother transitions, teaching behavioral expectations). Within 6 months, Jason's TPITOS scores had improved from 66% *Yes* to 88% *Yes*, with no Red Flags. Jason's and Sarah's coaching relationship continued beyond this 6-month observation with regular meetings and e-mail contact (see Figures 6.2 and 6.3).

Total Number of Red Flags Observed

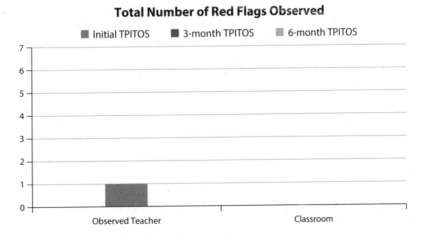

Figure 6.3.   Jason's 6-month TPITOS Red Flag scores.

They discussed how to maintain the changes Jason had made and identified additional goals to continue to work on over the next 6 months. They updated their action plan and continued working together to implement the *Pyramid Model* practices in Jason's classroom.

CASE STUDY 2: LITTLE BADGERS CHILD LEARNING CENTER: USING THE TPITOS TO PLAN PROGRAMWIDE IMPLEMENTATION OF THE *PYRAMID MODEL*

Little Badgers Child Learning Center (LBCLC) is a child care center for children 6 weeks to 5 years old. LBCLC serves 72 children in six classrooms. The program works with Individuals with Disabilities Education Act (IDEA)/Part C to provide early intervention services (e.g., occupational therapy) to children with disabilities and serves a large number of refugee families. The center also accepts subsidies from the local Child Care Resource and Referral (CCRR) network to support those families who lack the means to pay for child care. A mental health consultant, Alejandro, spends 10 hours per week at the center to support positive social and behavioral outcomes and visits families in their homes to promote better family functioning. The teachers in this program range in experience and education—all have a high school diploma, several have a bachelor's degree (a few of which are focused on education), and one teacher has a master's degree in art history. A handful of the teachers are working at the center to offset the high costs of child care. Each classroom has a lead teacher and at least one assistant. The classrooms for infants and toddlers have two assistants and 8–10 children per classroom. Alejandro provides much of the professional development to teachers.

LBCLC is accredited by the National Association for the Education of Young Children, and the director the of the center, Jasmine, has become particularly interested in addressing challenging behavior and supporting the social-emotional outcomes of young children, given the increasing number of children expelled because of behavior challenges. Teachers have also voiced this as a top concern to Jasmine, and Alejandro has been spending much of his time attempting to guide teachers in setting up the physical arrangement of the classroom and having effective routines to support children's social-emotional competence as well as talking with concerned parents. In addition to the expulsion issue, Jasmine has noticed many children who are transitioning from toddler to preschool classrooms have difficulty expressing their feelings and have trouble engaging in the daily classroom activities. This is evidenced by recent TPOT observations done by Alejandro in preschool classrooms.

Recently, Jasmine contacted her local child care resource and referral (CCRR) agency to inquire about professional development options to address the above-mentioned challenges and also asked Alejandro for input. The *Pyramid Model* for infants and toddlers was suggested by both her CCRR representative and Alejandro, because this approach would provide teachers with strategies that specifically target these types of difficulties. Upon sharing the news of the model and the TPITOS with his teachers and witnessing their subsequent enthusiasm, Jasmine soon contacted the Pyramid Consortium to inquire about TPITOS trainings. Upon doing so, training on the *Pyramid Model* was scheduled for teachers at this program and others in the area. Additionally, a TPITOS reliability certification training was scheduled for Jasmine, Alejandro, and the center IDEA/Part C early interventionist, Harlan, as well as other local allied health service providers and child care administrators.

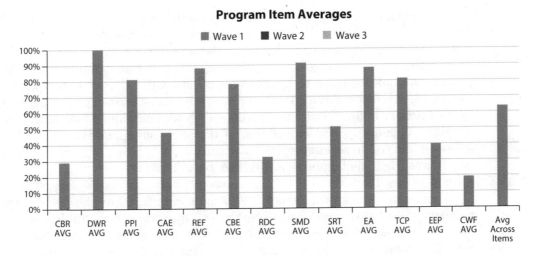

Figure 6.4. Little Badgers' initial TPITOS Indicator scores across six classrooms.

This certification training would allow them to begin observing the current level of practices used to support social-emotional development and start identifying and addressing areas of need. After successfully meeting the 80% reliability criteria with one of the developers of the TPITOS, all three were able to administer the measure in LBCLC classrooms. Alejandro and Harlan conducted the initial TPITOS observation with each teacher and then took advantage of the available Microsoft Excel TPITOS Spreadsheet to determine the average TPITOS Item scores and Red Flags across classrooms (see Figure 6.4).

The results of the summary brought to light the areas of need related to the implementation of the Pyramid practices. As a group, they decided to focus professional development activities on Tier 1 of the *Pyramid Model*: nurturing and responsive relationships and high-quality supportive environments (i.e., universal supports of the *Pyramid Model*). Practices within Tier 1 that were infrequent across classrooms included 1) providing opportunities for communication and building relationships (CBR), 2) responding to children in distress and managing challenging behaviors (RDC), and 3) using effective strategies for communicating with families and promoting family involvement in the classroom (CWF). In addition, the use of punitive practices was a Red Flag evident in three of the classrooms. Upon identifying these areas, and because several of teachers did not have a child development/education background, an initial workshop took place in order to provide an overview of appropriate infant–toddler practices. Coaching, using the approach described in the first case study, took place every other week with individual teachers. The coach and teacher worked together to identify shared goals and develop an action plan. The coaching team conducted focused observations and followed up with teachers in coaching sessions conducted every other week.

After 3 months, progress at the individual teacher and program level was assessed by administering a follow-up TPITOS with each teacher. Ample progress was made across classrooms in the initial goals (e.g., communication and relationship building [CBR], responding to distress and challenging behavior [RDC], and communicating with families and promoting family involvement [CWF]). So the team decided to turn its attention to other areas of need identified through teachers' input and TPITOS data: 1) conveying predictability through carefully planned schedule, routines, and transitions (SRT), and 2) promoting children's active engagement (CAE). In addition, during one of Jasmine's, Harlan's, and Alejandro's debriefing meetings, they realized that many of the teachers were still indicating a need for strategies to promote family involvement in the classroom. Again, the LBCLC Pyramid Model coaching team provided a brief workshop to familiarize teachers with evidence-based practices in these areas and discuss as a group the center's practices and policies relating to family involvement in the classroom. The coaching team continued individual coaching to ensure high-fidelity implementation of the universal supports and conducted a follow-up TPITOS to assess progress over time.

It was clear that improvements had been made in conveying predictability through planned schedules (SRT), promoting children's active engagement (CAE), and promoting family involvement (CWF; see Figure 6.5), but observers noted that teachers' use of strategies to promote smooth transitions was still infrequent, and the Red Flag related to use of punitive practices (e.g., speaking in a harsh tone) had resurfaced during these transition times (see Figure 6.6). To more systematically address this concern, the coaching team supplemented the existing professional development and coaching plan for the teachers struggling in these areas. They increased coaching to once a week temporarily. They also facilitated allowing the teachers to observe other classrooms where transitions were implemented effectively and where they could observe teachers addressing challenging situations using Pyramid practices (e.g., using a challenging situation to help children recognize and deal with emotions). Finally, they set aside time during the week for teachers to come together and discuss strategy use and the resulting progress and/or unexpected challenges. A subsequent TPITOS observation confirmed what the coaching team had been observing during more frequent focused observations—that teachers' practices had improved on implementing transitions (SRT) and reducing harsh talk directed toward children and that past improvements had also been sustained.

As improvements in TPITOS scores were maintained over time, TPITOS observations continued on a quarterly basis and the Tier 1 practices they targeted improved, resulting in positive changes in children's social-emotional skills, as well as

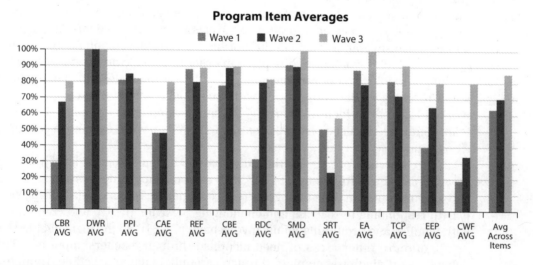

Figure 6.5. Little Badgers' 6-month TPITOS Indicator scores across six classrooms.

Program Red Flag Averages

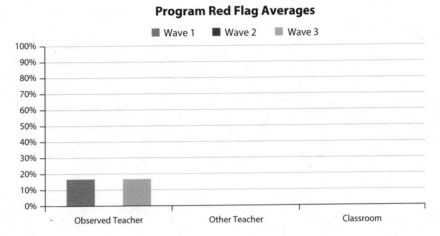

Figure 6.6. Little Badgers' 6-month TPITOS Red Flag scores across six classrooms.

the overall quality of the program. The coaching team continued to refine the coaching and professional development framework they had been implementing to ensure its sustainability within the program and to be responsive to the needs of the teachers and the program. They sought out feedback from teachers and used this feedback to improve their coaching and professional development efforts. Because of the success of this model, the program leadership made a commitment to continue to support this process by allocating time and resources to coaching as well as additional professional development and by seeking out additional professional development opportunities for staff and coaches.

References

Brauner, C. B., & Stephens, B. C. (2006). Estimating the prevalence of early childhood serious emotional/behavioral disorder: Challenges and recommendations. *Public Health Reports, 121,* 303–310. doi: 10.1177/003335490612100314.

Brown, C. M., Copeland, K. A., Sucharew, H., & Kahn, R. S. (2012). Social-emotional problems in preschool-aged children: Opportunities for prevention and early intervention. *Archives of Pediatrics & Adolescent Medicine, 166*(10), 926–932.

Cabaj, J. L., McDonald, S. W., & Tough, S. C. (2014). Early childhood risk and resilience factors for behavioural and emotional problems in middle childhood. *BMC Pediatrics, 14,* 166. doi: 10.1186/1471-2431-14-166.

Campbell, F. A., Pungello, E. P., Miller-Johnson, S., Burchinal, M. & Ramey, C. T. (2001). The development of cognitive and academic abilities: Growth curves from an early childhood educational experiment. *Developmental Psychology, 37*(2), 231–242.

Center on Social and Emotional Foundations for Early Learning at Vanderbilt University. (2003). *Pyramid Model for promoting social and emotional competence in infants and young children.* Nashville, TN: Author.

Child Trends Databank. (2014). *Early childhood program enrollment.* Retrieved from Child Trends website https://www.childtrends.org/?indicators=early-childhood-program-enrollment

Cooper, J. L., Masi, R., & Vick, J. (2009). *Social-emotional development in early childhood: What every policymaker should know.* New York, NY: National Center for Children in Poverty.

Copple, C., & Bredekamp, S. (2009). *Developmentally appropriate practice in early childhood programs serving children from birth through age 8.* Washington, DC: National Association for the Education of Young Children.

Division for Early Childhood. (2014). *DEC recommended practices in early intervention/early childhood special education 2014.* Retrieved from http://www.dec-sped.org/dec-recommended-practices

Duncan, G. J., & Brooks-Gunn, J. (2000). Family poverty, welfare reform, and child development. *Child Development, 71*(1), 188–196.

Duncan, G. J., Brooks-Gunn, J., & Klebanov, P. K. (1994). Economic deprivation and early childhood development. *Child Development, 65*(2), 296–318.

Fox, L., Dunlap, G., Hemmeter, M. L., Joseph, G. E., & Strain, P. S. (2003). The Teaching Pyramid: A model for supporting social competence and preventing challenging behavior in young children. *Young Children, 58*(4), 48–52.

Fox, L., Hemmeter, M. L., & Snyder, P. S. (2014). *Teaching Pyramid Observation Tool (TPOT™) for Preschool Classrooms, Research Edition.* Baltimore, MD: Paul H. Brookes Publishing Co.

Gordon Jr., R. S. (1983). An operational classification of disease prevention. *Public Health Reports, 98*(2), 107–109.

Guttentag, C. L., Landry, S. H., Williams, J. M., Baggett, K. M., Noria, C. W., Borkowski, J. G., . . . & Carta, J. J. (2014). "My Baby & Me": Effects of an early, comprehensive parenting intervention on at-risk mothers and their children. *Developmental Psychology, 50*(5), 1482–1496.

Hemmeter, M. L., Fox, L., Snyder, P., & Algina, J. (2016, April). *Research on the Pyramid Model.* Paper presented at the annual meeting of the National Training Institute on Young Children with Challenging Behavior, Tampa, FL.

Hemmeter, M. L., Ostrosky, M., & Fox, L. (2006). Social and emotional foundations for early learning: A conceptual model for intervention. *School Psychology Review, 35*(4), 583–601.

Hemmeter, M. L., Snyder, P., Fox, L., & Algina, J. (2011, April). *Efficacy of a classroom wide model for promoting social-emotional development and preventing challenging behavior.* Paper presented at the annual meeting of the American Educational Research Association, New Orleans, LA.

Hemmeter, M. L., Snyder, P., Fox, L., & Algina, J. (2016). The efficacy of the Pyramid Model: Effects on teachers, classrooms, and children. *Topics in Early Childhood Special Education.* Advance online publication. doi:10.1177/0271121416653386.

Horner, R. H., Sugai, G., Todd, A. W., Lewis-Palmer, T., Bambara, L., & Kern, L. (2005). School-wide positive behavior support. In L. Bambara & L. Kern (Eds.) *Individualized supports for students with problem behaviors: Designing positive behavior plans.* (pp. 359–390). New York, NY: Guilford Press.

Landry, S. H., Smith, K. E., Swank, P. R., & Guttentag, C. (2008). A responsive parenting intervention: The optimal timing across early childhood for impacting maternal behaviors and child outcomes. *Developmental Psychology, 44*(5), 1335–1353.

National Center on Quality Teaching and Learning. (2013). *What do we know about coaching? (issues brief).* Retrieved from https://eclkc.ohs.acf.hhs.gov/sites/default/files/pdf/pbc-what-do-we-know.pdf

National Research Council & Institute of Medicine. (2000). From neurons to neighborhoods: The science of early child development. Committee on Integrating the Science of Early Childhood Development. In J. P. Shonkoff, & D. A. Phillips (Eds.), *Board on children, youth, and families, commission on behavioral and social sciences and education.* Washington, DC: National Academy Press.

Schnitz, A. G., Hardy, J. K., Artman, K. M., & Hemmeter, M. L. (2013). Helping teachers implement the Pyramid Model using practice-based coaching [Monograph]. *Young Exceptional Children, 15,* 95–110.

Simeonsson, R. J. (1991). Primary, secondary, and tertiary prevention in early intervention. *Journal of Early Intervention, 15*(2), 124–134.

Snyder, P., Hemmeter, M. L., & Fox, L. (2015). Supporting implementation of evidence-based practices through practice-based coaching. *Topics in Early Childhood Special Education, 35,* 1–11. doi: 10.1177/0271121415594925.

U.S. Department of Health and Human Services & U.S. Department of Education. (2015). *Policy statement on expulsion and suspension policies in early childhood settings.* Retrieved from http://www2.ed.gov/policy/gen/guid/school-discipline/policy-statement-ece-expulsions-suspensions.pdf

Key to Teaching Pyramid Infant–Toddler Observation Scale Items and Abbreviations

Item Number and Abbreviation	Item Name
1. CBR	Teacher provides opportunities for **C**ommunication and **B**uilding **R**elationships
2. DWR	Teacher **D**emonstrates **W**armth and **R**esponsivity to individual children
3. PPI	Teacher promotes **P**ositive **P**eer **I**nteractions
4. CAE	Teacher promotes **C**hildren's **A**ctive **E**ngagement
5. REF	Teacher is **R**esponsive to children's expression of **E**motions and teaches about **F**eelings
6. CBE	Teacher **C**ommunicates and provides feedback about developmentally appropriate **B**ehavioral **E**xpectations
7. RDC	Teacher **R**esponds to children in **D**istress and manages **C**hallenging behaviors
8. SMD	Teacher uses specific **S**trategies or **M**odifications for children with **D**isabilities/delays, or who are dual language learners
9. SRT	Teacher conveys predictability through carefully planned **S**chedule, **R**outines, and **T**ransitions
10. EA	**E**nvironment is **A**rranged to foster social-emotional development
11. TCP	**T**eacher **C**ollaborates with his or her **P**eers (e.g., other teachers, mental health practitioners, allied health professionals) to support children's social-emotional development
12. EEP	Teacher has **E**ffective strategies for **E**ngaging **P**arents in supporting their children's social-emotional development and addressing challenging behaviors
13. CWF	Teacher has effective strategies for **C**ommunicating **W**ith **F**amilies and promoting family involvement in the classroom

89

Appendix B

Indicators That Can Be Scored *Not Applicable*

The specific Indicators for which observers have the option of scoring *Not Applicable (N/A)* are listed below. The first section lists Indicators that can be scored *N/A* because there was not an opportunity to observe the behavior. The second section lists Indicators that can be scored *N/A* specifically because toddlers were not present. Some Indicators may be listed in both sections.

INDICATORS THAT CAN BE SCORED *N/A* IF NO OPPORTUNITY TO OBSERVE

CBR8. Teacher uses alternative strategies for communicating with children who have language delays or are DLLs. **Mark *N/A* if children who have language delays or are DLLs are not enrolled.**

PPI6. Teacher offers comfort when negative social interactions occur among children. **Score *N/A* if there are no negative social interactions observed.**

PPI7. Teacher models social skills for children, such as sharing, gentle touching, requesting, or using words. **Score *N/A* if modeling was not the appropriate strategy.**

CAE5. Adults in the room work together to make sure all children are engaged. **Score *N/A* if only one teacher is present.**

REF6. Teacher uses real-life classroom situations to identify feelings and problem-solve when <u>toddlers</u> have conflicts or when <u>toddlers</u> experience frustration. **Score *N/A* if there are no situations in which this could be scored or there are no toddlers present.**

CBE5. Teacher uses simple words or phrases to explain natural consequences of engaging in unsafe behavior. **Mark *N/A* if unsafe behavior is not observed.**

CBE6. Teacher provides feedback to <u>toddlers</u> in instances of behavior that does not meet classroom expectations. **Mark *N/A* if there are no instances of behavior not meeting classroom expectations or there are no toddlers present.**

RDC1. Teacher's tone remains calm, supportive, and positive during children's distressful or challenging episodes. **Score *N/A* if there are no instances of child distress or challenging behavior.**

RDC2. Teacher immediately responds to children in distress to assess children's status. **Score *N/A* if there are no instances of child distress.**

RDC3. Teacher provides positive attention to <u>toddlers</u> when they have calmed down and are behaving appropriately. **Score *N/A* if there are no instances of child distress or challenging behavior among toddlers or there are no toddlers present.**

RDC4. Teacher uses a challenging situation as an opportunity to help children recognize and deal with emotions. **Score *N/A* if there are no opportunities to observe how the teacher uses challenging situations as a teaching opportunity.**

RDC5. Teacher provides support to <u>toddlers</u> who are angry or upset to help them with problem solving, when appropriate. **Score *N/A* if there are no instances of child distress or challenging behavior or there are no toddlers present.**

RDC6. Teacher uses strategies such as redirection and/or planned ignoring with individual <u>toddlers</u> who are in distress or engage in occasional episodes of challenging behavior. **Score *N/A* if there are no instances of child distress or challenging behavior or when there are no toddlers present.**

RDC7. Teacher uses a variety of strategies to console, soothe, or calm children who are in distress and individualizes responses according to children and situations. **Score *N/A* if there are no instances of child distress.**

SMD1. Teacher reports using specific strategies or modifications to support the social-emotional development of children with disabilities/delays. **Score *N/A* if there are no children who require specific modifications.**

SMD2. Teacher reports using specific strategies or modifications to promote social-emotional development with children who are DLLs. **Score *N/A* if there are no children who require specific modifications with regard to dual languages.**

SRT3. During group transitions for <u>toddlers</u>, teacher uses verbal and/or visual cues and a predictable routine that minimizes excessive waiting. **Mark *N/A* if you do not see group transitions or if there are no toddlers present.**

SRT5. Before a transition to a new activity, teacher conveys in developmentally and individually appropriate ways information about what <u>toddlers</u> should expect. **Mark *N/A* if you do not see group transitions or if there are no toddlers present.**

EA3. In rooms for <u>infants</u> younger than 12 months, there is open space for <u>infants</u> to have "tummy time." **Score *N/A* if there are no *infants* younger than 12 months.**

EA4. In rooms for <u>toddlers</u> who are capable of running, traffic patterns in the classroom are arranged so that there are no wide open spaces for running. **Score *N/A* if no toddlers are present.**

TCP1. Almost all interactions in the classroom between the teacher and his or her peers are related to children or classroom activities. **Score *N/A* if no other adults are present.**

TCP5. Teacher describes ways in which he or she has shared information and communicated with allied health professionals (e.g., PT, OT). **Score *N/A* if the teacher has not or does not currently have the opportunity to communicate with other professionals regarding children within the classroom.**

TCP6. Teacher reports incorporating information communicated by or with other members of the team and with parents into classroom practices to ensure all needs are met. **Score *N/A* if the teacher has not or does not currently have the opportunity to communicate with other professionals regarding children within the classroom.**

EEP5. When a <u>toddler</u> has significant behavior challenges, teacher indicates that he or she works together with the family and other mental health support services to develop and implement a behavior support plan. **Score *N/A* if there are no significant behavior challenges with a behavior support plan or there are no toddlers present.**

INDICATORS THAT CAN BE SCORED *N/A* IF THERE ARE NO TODDLERS PRESENT

PPI4. Teacher helps <u>toddlers</u> work cooperatively during activities/routines.

CAE4. Teacher provides <u>toddlers</u> with opportunities to make choices.

REF3. Teacher points out peers' words, voice tone, or facial expressions to help <u>toddlers</u> recognize and understand emotions.

REF6. Teacher uses real-life classroom situations to identify feelings and problem-solve when <u>toddlers</u> have conflicts or when <u>toddlers</u> experience frustration.

CBE2. Teacher communicates behavioral expectations by letting <u>toddlers</u> know, in a positive tone, what they should do in specific activities (and not just what they shouldn't do).

CBE6. Teacher provides feedback to <u>toddlers</u> in instances of behavior that does not meet classroom expectations.

RDC3. Teacher provides positive attention to <u>toddlers</u> when they have calmed down and are behaving appropriately.

RDC5. Teacher provides support to <u>toddlers</u> who are angry or upset to help them with problem solving, when appropriate.

RDC6. Teacher uses strategies such as redirection and/or planned ignoring with individual <u>toddlers</u> who are in distress or engage in occasional episodes of challenging behavior.

SRT3. During group transitions for <u>toddlers</u>, teacher uses verbal and/or visual cues and a predictable routine that minimizes excessive waiting.

SRT5. Before a transition to a new activity, teacher conveys in developmentally and individually appropriate ways information about what <u>toddlers</u> should expect.

EA4. In rooms for <u>toddlers</u> who are capable of running, traffic patterns in the classroom are arranged so that there are no wide open spaces for running.

EEP5. When a <u>toddler</u> has significant behavior challenges, teacher indicates that he or she works together with the family and other mental health support services to develop and implement a behavior support plan.

Indicators with Scoring Criteria Regarding Frequency of Observed Behavior

The following list of Indicators specify frequency of behaviors in the scoring criteria (e.g., more than one) or include the criterion to observe a *variety* of strategies or practices. When variety is stated within the scoring criteria, this refers to the criteria that at least two of the strategies or practices were observed or reported.

Indicators with scoring criteria regarding frequency of observed behavior

Indicator	Elaboration
PPI3. Teacher encourages children to initiate or maintain interactions with their peers during activities and routines.	To score *Yes*, you should see at least two occasions of the teacher helping children initiate/maintain interactions with their peers. Score *No* if you see *fewer than two instances* of the teacher helping a child initiate/maintain an interaction with a peer.
PPI5. Teacher provides positive descriptive comments to children who are engaging in positive peer interactions.	To score *Yes*, you should hear the teacher support peer-to-peer interactions through positive statements on *two occasions*. Score *No* if the teacher fails to acknowledge a child's positive behavior toward a peer on *two occasions*.
PPI9. Teacher uses a variety (i.e., more than one) of developmentally appropriate strategies and/or materials (e.g., books, puppets) to encourage peer-to-peer interactions. **Interview Question:** "What types of strategies and/or materials do you use to promote positive peer interactions?"	To score *Yes*, you should observe the teacher supporting child-to-child positive interactions through a variety of strategies and/or materials. Score *No* if materials and activities that can support children's peer relations are available and the teacher does not make use of them or does not use a *variety* of strategies for encouraging interaction.
CAE1. Teacher makes positive and varied attempts to encourage unengaged children to become engaged in an activity.	Score *No* if you see unengaged children and the teacher does not initiate *one or more attempts* to engage children.
CAE2. Teacher uses a variety of ways to help children sustain their engagement in an activity.	Score *Yes* if the teacher is observed adjusting an activity, such as by introducing novelty or making slight changes to the activity or by using a variety of prompts to re-engage a child who might have become disengaged. Score *No* if the teacher shows no evidence of using a *variety* of ways to sustain engagement in an activity.

(continued)

(continued)

Indicator	Elaboration
CAE4. N/A Teacher provides <u>toddlers</u> with opportunities to make choices.	Score *Yes* if the teacher provides a child or multiple children with *at least two choices* during the routine observed. Score *No* if choices were offered fewer than two times by the teacher.
REF7. Teacher uses a variety of strategies to teach children about feeling words. **Interview Question:** "What strategies do you use to teach feeling words (e.g., role play, feelings chart)?"	Teacher uses strategies to teach feeling words that are varied, and/or uses them across a *variety* of activities or situations. Score *Yes* if the teacher introduces feeling words using a *variety* of strategies. Score *No* if the teacher does not talk or teach about feeling words *in a variety of ways*.
RDC6. N/A Teacher uses strategies such as redirection and/or planned ignoring with individual <u>toddlers</u> who are in distress or engage in occasional episodes of challenging behavior. **Interview Question:** "Tell me what strategies you follow when children have occasional episodes of challenging behavior (e.g., physical aggression, screaming, taking others' toys)?"	Score *Yes* if you observe the teacher attempting to calmly use redirection and/or planned ignoring (e.g., consciously choosing to not reinforce or attend to an undesirable behavior) in response to distress or challenging behavior. Score *No* if the teacher does not use a *variety* of strategies in response to children who are upset or in distress or if the teacher uses the same strategy in all situations.
SMD2. N/A Teacher uses or reports using specific strategies or modifications to promote social-emotional development with children who are dual language learners (DLLs). **Interview Question:** "Can you describe any specific strategies, modifications, activities, or materials you use with children who are DLLs to promote social-emotional development?"	If more than one language is spoken by children in the room, the teacher should note how he or she uses strategies or modifications with *at least two different children.*
EA1. Early learning environment includes a variety of developmentally appropriate toys and play areas to support engagement and social interaction.	*A variety* of toys are available to meet the developmental needs of every child in the classroom. Score *No* if *a variety* of toys and play areas that can be used in supporting engagement or interaction are not present.
TCP5. N/A Teacher describes ways in which he or she has shared information and communicated with allied health professionals (e.g., PT, OT). **Interview Question:** "Do you communicate with allied health professionals (e.g., PT, OT) about any children in your classroom? If so, how do you go about sharing information and getting the information you need?"	Score *No* if the teacher does not describe any examples of having shared information with team members or parents, or if the examples were *one time instances and not a frequent practice.* If a teacher reports on communication with parents only and not with professionals, score *No*.
CWF5. Teacher describes a variety of strategies for promoting family involvement in the classroom. **Interview Question:** "Tell me about what you do to promote family involvement in your classroom (e.g., help families feel welcome, get them involved, gain trust, offer choices for ways to engage)."	Score *Yes* if the teacher indicates a *variety* of differentiated approaches to support caregiver involvement in the classroom on a regular basis. Score *No* if there is only one strategy to promote family involvement or if the opportunities for involvement are limited to just infrequent, special events.

Related Readings and Resources

PYRAMID MODEL AND STRATEGIES FOR PROMOTING SOCIAL-EMOTIONAL DEVELOPMENT OF YOUNG CHILDREN

Carta, J. J., Greenwood, C. R., Luze, G. J., Cline, G., & Kuntz, S. (2004). Developing a general outcome measure of growth in social skills for infants and toddlers. *Journal of Early Intervention, 26,* 91–114. doi: 10.1177/02711214020220030201

Carta, J. J., & Young, R. M., (in press). *Multi-tiered systems of support for young children: Driving change in early education.* Baltimore, MD: Paul H. Brookes Publishing Co.

Cohen, J., Onunaku, N., Clothier, S., & Poppe, J. (2005). *Helping young children succeed: Strategies to promote early childhood social and emotional development.* Retrieved from http://www .buildinitiative.org/WhatsNew/ViewArticle/tabid/96/ArticleId/396/Helping-Young-Children-Succeed-Strategies-to-Promote-Early-Childhood-Social-and-Emotional-Developmen.aspx

Conroy, M. (2004). Early identification, prevention, and early intervention for young children at risk for emotional, behavior disorders: Issues, trends, and a call to action. *Behavioral Disorders, 29*(3), 224–236.

Conroy, M. A., Sutherland, K. S., Vo, A. K., Carr, S., & Ogston, P. L. (2014). Early childhood teachers' use of effective instructional practices and the collateral effects on young children's behavior. *Journal of Positive Behavior Interventions, 16*(2), 81–92.

Cutler, A., & Gilkerson, L. (2006). *Unmet needs project: A research, coalition building, and policy initiative on the unmet needs of infants, toddlers, and families–Final report.* Retrieved from https://www.illinois.gov/icdd/Documents/Comm/Unmet-Needs-Final-Report.pdf

Denham, S. A., Blair, K. A., DeMulder, E., Levitas, J., Sawyer, K., Auerbach–Major, S., & Queenan, P. (2003). Preschool emotional competence: Pathway to social competence? *Child Development, 74*(1), 238–256.

Dunlap, G., Strain, P. S., Fox, L., Carta, J., Conroy, M., Smith, B., . . . Sowell, C. (2006). Prevention and intervention with young children's challenging behavior: Perspectives regarding current knowledge. *Behavioral Disorders, 32*(1), 29–45.

Dunlap, G., Strain, P., Lee, J., Joseph, J., & Leech, N. (2017). *A randomized controlled evaluation of prevent-teach-reinforce for young children.* Manuscript accepted for publication.

Dunlap, G., Strain, P. S., Lee, J., Joseph, J., Vatland, C., & Fox, L. (2017). *Prevent-teach-reinforce for families: A model of positive behavior support for home and community.* Baltimore, MD: Paul H. Brookes Publishing Co.

Dunlap, G., Wilson, K., Strain, P., & Lee, J. (2013). *Prevent-teach-reinforce for young children: The early childhood model of individualized positive behavior support.* Baltimore, MD: Paul H. Brookes Publishing Co.

Fox, L., Dunlap, G., Hemmeter, M. L., Joseph, G., & Strain, G. (2003). The Teaching Pyramid: A model for supporting social competence and preventing challenging behavior in young children. *Young Children, 58*(4), 48–53.

Fox, L., Hemmeter, M. L., & Snyder, P. S. (2014). *Teaching Pyramid Observation Tool for Preschool Classrooms (TPOT™) for preschool classrooms, research edition.* Baltimore, MD: Paul H. Brookes Publishing Co.

Fox, L., Veguilla, M., & Perez-Binder, D. (2014). *Data decision-making and program-wide implementation of the Pyramid Model. Roadmap to effective intervention practices #7.* Tampa, FL: University of South Florida, Technical Assistance Center on Social Emotional Intervention for Young Children.

Gloeckler, L., & Niemeyer, J. (2010). Social emotional environments: Teacher practices in two toddler classrooms. *Early Childhood Research to Practice, 12*(1), 1–9. Retrieved from http://ecrp.uiuc.edu/v12n1/gloeckler.html

Hardy, J. K., Brown, J., Skow, K., & the IRIS Center. (2015). Early childhood behavior management. Retrieved from http://www.iris.peabody.vanderbilt.edu/wp-content/uploads/pdf_case_studies/ics_behaviormgmt.pdf

Hemmeter, M. L., & Conroy, M. (2012). Supporting the social competence of young children with challenging behavior in the context of the Teaching Pyramid model: Research-based practices and implementation in early childhood settings. In R. Pianta, L. Justice, S. Barnett, & S. Sheridan (Eds.), *The handbook of early education* (pp. 416–434). New York, NY: Guilford Press.

Hemmeter, M. L., Fox, L., & Hardy, J. K. (2016). Supporting the implementation of tiered models of behavior support in early childhood settings. In B. R. Reichow, B. Boyd, E. Barton, & S. Odom (Eds.), *Handbook of early childhood education* (pp. 247–265). New York, NY: Springer Publishing.

Hemmeter, M. L., Fox, L., & Snyder, P. (2013). A tiered model for promoting social-emotional competence and addressing challenging behavior. In V. Buysse & E. Peisner-Feinberg (Eds.), *Handbook of response to intervention in early childhood* (pp. 85–101). Baltimore, MD: Paul H. Brookes Publishing Co.

Hemmeter, M. L., Fox, L., & Snyder, P. (2014). *Teaching Pyramid Observation Tool (TPOT™) for preschool classrooms manual, research edition.* Baltimore, MD: Paul H. Brookes Publishing Co.

Hemmeter, M. L., Fox, L., Strain, P., Hardy, J. K., & Joseph, J. (in press). How do we design and implement Tier 2 instructional support to promote social-emotional outcomes and prevent challenging behaviors? In J. Carta & R. M. Young (Eds.), *Multi-tiered systems of support for young children: A guide to response to intervention in early education.*

Hemmeter, M. L., Ostrosky, M., & Corso, R. (2012). Preventing and addressing challenging behavior: Common questions and practical solutions. *Young Exceptional Children, 15,* 31–44. doi: 10.1177/1096250611427350.

Hemmeter, M. L., Ostrosky, M., & Fox, L. (2006). Social and emotional foundations for early learning: A conceptual model for intervention. *School Psychology Review, 35*(4), 583–601.

Hemmeter, M. L., Snyder, P. A., Fox, L., & Algina, J. (2016). Evaluating the implementation of the Pyramid Model for promoting social-emotional competence in early childhood classrooms. *Topics in Early Childhood Special Education, 36*(3), 133–146.

Hunter, A., & Hemmeter, M. L. (2009). The Center on the Social and Emotional Foundations for Early Learning: Addressing challenging behaviors in infants and toddlers. *Zero to Three, 29*(3), 5–12.

Institute of Medicine. (2000). *From neurons to neighborhoods: The science of early childhood development.* Washington, DC: National Academy Press.

Joseph, G. E., & Strain, P. S. (2003). Enhancing emotional vocabulary in young children. *Young Exceptional Children, 6*(4), 18–26.

National Scientific Council on the Developing Child. (2004). *Young children develop in an environment of relationships: Working paper no. 1.* Retrieved from http://developingchild.harvard.edu/library/reports_and_working papers/working papers/wp1/

National Survey of Early Care and Education Project Team. (2013). *Number and Characteristics of Early Care and Education (ECE) Teachers and Caregivers: Initial Findings from the National Survey of Early Care and Education (NSECE). OPRE Report #2013-38.* Washington, DC: Office of Planning, Research and Evaluation, Administration for Children and Families, U.S. Department of Health and Human Services.

Shonkoff, J. P., Garner, A., & the Committee on Psychosocial Aspects of Child and Family Health, Committee on Early Childhood, Adoption, and Dependent Care, and Section on Developmental and Behavioral Pediatrics. (2012). The lifelong effects of early childhood adversity and toxic stress. *Pediatrics, 129,* 232–246. doi: 10.1542/eds.2011-2663.

Snyder, P., Hemmeter, M. L., & Fox, L. (2015). Supporting implementation of evidence-based practices through practice-based coaching. *Topics in Early Childhood Special Education, 35,* 1–11. doi: 10.1177/0271121415594925.

Snyder, P., Hemmeter, M. L., McLean, M., & Sandall, S. (2013). Embedded instruction at Tier 2. In V. Buysse & E. Peisner-Feinberg (Eds.), *Handbook of response to intervention in early intervention.* Baltimore, MD: Paul H. Brookes Publishing Co.

Snyder, P. A., Hemmeter, M. L., Fox, L., Bishop, C. C., & Miller, M. D. (2013). Developing and gathering psychometric evidence for a fidelity instrument: The Teaching Pyramid Observation Tool–Pilot version. *Journal of Early Intervention, 35,* 150–172. doi: 10.1177/1053815113516794.

Snyder, P. A., Rakap, S., Hemmeter, M. L., McLaughlin, T. W., Sandall, S., & McLean, M. E. (2015). Naturalistic instructional approaches in early learning: A systematic review. *Journal of Early Intervention, 37*, 60–97. doi: 1053815115595461.

Squires, J., & Bricker, D. (2007). *An activity-based approach for developing children's social-emotional competence.* Baltimore, MD: Paul H. Brookes Publishing Co.

Squires, J., Bricker, D., Waddell, M., Funk, K., Clifford, J., & Hoselton, R. (2014). *Social- Emotional Assessment/Evaluation Measure (SEAM™), research edition.* Baltimore, MD: Paul H. Brooks Publishing Co.

Strain, P. S., & Joseph, G. E. (2006). You've got to have friends: Promoting friendships for preschool children. *Young Exceptional Children Monograph Series, 8*, 57–66.

Vinh, M., Strain, P., Davidon, S., & Smith, B. J. (2016). One state's systems change efforts to reduce child care expulsion: Taking the Pyramid Model to scale. *Topics in Early Childhood Special Education, 36*, 159–164. doi: 10.1177/0271121415626130.

PROFESSIONAL DEVELOPMENT AND COACHING

Artman, K. & Hemmeter, M. L. (2013). Effects of training and feedback on teachers' use of classroom preventive practices. *Topics in Early Childhood Special Education, 13*, 112–123. doi: 10.1177/0271121412447115.

Artman, K., Hemmeter, M. L., & Snyder, P. (2014). Effects of distance coaching on teachers' use of Pyramid Model practices: A pilot study. *Infants and Young Children, 27*, 325–344. doi: 10.1097/IYC.0000000000000016.

Barton, E. E., Kinder, K., Casey, A. M., & Artman, K. M. (2011). Finding your feedback fit: Strategies for designing and delivering performance feedback systems. *Young Exceptional Children, 14*, 29–46. doi: 10.1177/1096250610395459.

Fettig, A., & Artman-Meeker, K. (2016). Group coaching on pre-school teachers' implementation of Pyramid Model strategies: A program description. *Topics in Early Childhood Special Education, 36*(3), 147–158.

Fox, L., & Hemmeter, M. L., (2011). Coaching early educators to implement effective practices. *Zero to Three, 32*(2), 18–24.

Fox, L., Hemmeter, M. L., Snyder, P., Binder, D., & Clarke, S. (2011). Coaching early childhood educators to implement a comprehensive model for the promotion of young children's social competence. *Topics in Early Childhood Special Education, 31*, 178–192. doi: 10.1177/0271121411404440.

Hemmeter, M. L., Hardy, J. K., Schnitz, A. G., Adams, J. M., & Kinder, K. A. (2015). Effects of training and coaching with performance feedback on teachers' use of Pyramid Model practices. *Topics in Early Childhood Special Education, 35*, 144–156. doi: 10.1177/0271121415594924.

Hemmeter, M. L., Snyder, P., Kinder, K., & Artman, K. (2011). Impact of performance feedback delivered via electronic mail on preschool teachers' use of descriptive praise. *Early Childhood Research Quarterly, 26*, 96–109. doi: 10.1016/j.ecresq.2010.05.004.

McLeod, R., Artman-Meeker, K., & Hardy, J. K. (2017). Preparing yourself for coaching: Partnering for success. *Young Children, 72*(3), 75–81.

Schnitz, A. G., Hardy, J. K., Artman, K. M., & Hemmeter, M. L. (2013). Helping teachers implement the Pyramid Model using practice-based coaching [Monograph]. *Young Exceptional Children, 15*, 95–110.

Snyder, P., Hemmeter, M. L., Artman, K., Kinder, K., Pasia, C., & McLaughlin, T. (2012). Characterizing key features of the early childhood professional development literature. *Infants and Young Children, 25*(3), 188–212.

Snyder, P., Hemmeter, M. L., & Fox, L. (2015). Supporting implementation of evidence-based practices through practice-based coaching. *Topics in Early Childhood Special Education, 35*, 1–11. doi: 10.1177/0271121415594925.

Steed, E. A., & Durand, V. M. (2013). Optimistic teaching: Improving the capacity for teachers to reduce young children's challenging behavior. *School Mental Health, 5*(1), 15–24.

The IRIS Center for Training Enhancements. (2014). *Early childhood behavior management: Developing and teaching rules.* Retrieved from http://iris.peabody.vanderbilt.edu/module/ecbm/

Winton, P. J., Snyder, P., & Goffin, S. (2016). Beyond the status quo: Rethinking professional development for early childhood teachers. In L. Couse & S. Recchia (Eds.), *Handbook of early childhood teacher education* (pp. 54–68). New York, NY: Routledge.

WEB SITES

Center for Early Childhood Mental Health Consultation Center

https://www.ecmhc.org

This web site was developed around the *Pyramid Model* and includes a variety of resources related to supporting staff in implementing the *Pyramid Model* practices. These resources include surveys, supports for supporting social emotional competence, tools for developing behavior plans for young children, a guide for selecting screening and assessment tools, materials for families and administers, and tools that mental health consultants or others who support teachers can use in their everyday work.

National Center for Pyramid Model Innovations

http://challengingbehavior.org

The National Center for Pyramid Model Innovations (NCPMI) provides training, technical assistance, and resources related to the implementation of the *Pyramid Model* within state systems and local programs. This web site provides access to all previously developed *Pyramid Model* training and implementation materials (including infant–toddler training modules and family engagement materials originally developed by CSEFEL) and will offer access to new resources related to inclusion, equity, family engagement, data tools, state implementation, and program-wide implementation. Some materials are available in Spanish.

Pyramid Model Consortium

http://www.pyramidmodel.org

Resources include online training modules related to implementing the *Pyramid Model*, modules for training family child care providers, tip sheets, resources related to preventing suspension and expulsion, fact sheets on *Pyramid Model* research, and many other resources for families, providers, administrators, and coaches. Information on TPITOS Reliability Trainings can also be found on this web site.

ZERO TO THREE

https://www.zerotothree.org

This web site includes a number of free resources and products for early childhood professionals, parents, and policymakers for promoting early childhood social–emotional development of infants and toddlers.

Frequently Asked Questions

1. HOW IS THE TPITOS DIFFERENT FROM OTHER CLASSROOM OBSERVATION TOOLS?

The TPITOS is a targeted tool that provides information on the use of specific evidence-informed practices related to social-emotional competence and focuses on specific teacher practices aimed at promoting social-emotional development in infant and toddler early childhood classroom settings. The observation is conducted with one teacher at a time in order to collect information that is specific to one teacher and can be used to inform coaching and professional development. Although there are some items that address how well teachers work together or work with other professionals, the TPITOS focuses specifically on the observed teacher's practices aimed at supporting social-emotional development and reducing challenging child behavior.

2. HOW IS THE TPITOS SIMILAR TO AND DIFFERENT FROM THE TEACHING PYRAMID OBSERVATION TOOL (TPOT)?

The format and structure of the TPITOS are very similar to that of the TPOT. In fact, much of that was intentional to support the use of both instruments in early childhood settings. They both assess the implementation of key practices associated with the *Pyramid Model* for promoting social-emotional development. They are both administered by trained observers, and observations are 2 hours in length. TPOT and TPITOS allow observers to score key practices based on observation and interview, are organized into specific items and Indicators, and both include Red Flags. The TPITOS, however, is focused on settings for children from birth to 3 years of age, whereas the TPOT focuses on preschool classrooms with children 2–5 years of age. The TPOT is a class-wide observation, whereas the TPITOS involves observing one teacher at a time. Finally, the TPITOS items are scored for each daily routine observed. TPITOS observers score teacher practices within at least three different routines, which might include play, structured group, personal care, and outdoor activities.

3. WHAT TIER OF THE PYRAMID DOES THE TPITOS ADDRESS?

The TPITOS primarily addresses the first, or Universal Practices tier of the *Pyramid Model*, focusing on nurturing and responsive relationships and high-quality early childhood environments that promote positive outcomes for all children.

4. WHO CAN ADMINISTER THE TPITOS?

The TPITOS should be administered by a trained observer. This can be achieved by attending a TPITOS training workshop, achieving 80% agreement with the master coder by scoring a 2-hour TPITOS video, and achieving the recommended interrater agreement criteria when using the TPITOS in the field on three occasions.

The TPITOS is generally administered by coaches, supervisors, master or mentor teachers, mental health consultants, education coordinators, Positive Behavior Intervention and Support coaches, or center directors. It is used by professionals who are providing support and coaching to infant–toddler program personnel and focused on improving practices to improve child social-emotional outcomes. We recommend that TPITOS observers understand and have experience with the *Pyramid Model* and in working in infant and toddler settings. It is important to have a solid understanding of Infant–Toddler Pyramid practices. At minimum, observers should have completed the Center on the Social and Emotional Foundations for Early Learning (CSEFEL) Infant/Toddler Modules (These can be obtained at http://challengingbehavior.org).

5. HOW LONG DOES IT TAKE TO ADMINISTER THE TPITOS?

Administration of the TPITOS includes a 2-hour classroom observation, followed by a 15- to 20-minute interview with the teacher who was observed. We recommend that you complete this 2-hour observation in one session and then conduct the interview shortly thereafter. Scoring then takes an additional 30–45 minutes.

6. WHY IS THE TPITOS CONDUCTED ACROSS DIFFERENT ROUTINES?

In infant–toddler classrooms, teachers typically spend their time in very different activities throughout the day as they respond to the individual needs of infants and toddlers. In most cases, co-teachers divide their attention among differing routines, such that one teacher is diapering or feeding, while another is playing on the floor with other children, and yet another teacher is engaging in a small, structured group activity. It may be the case that a teacher excels during certain types of routines but could improve practices in other routines. By observing each teacher across multiple routines, the opportunity to identify areas of strengths and weaknesses is increased. This information is then used to inform coaching and professional development, which can be tailored to not only specific practices but also routines.

7. HOW DO I OBSERVE WHEN A CLASSROOM INCLUDES INFANTS AND TODDLERS?

The TPITOS Items and Indicators were designed to be inclusive of practices appropriate for infant and toddler care settings. In some cases, however, there are some practices that are more appropriate for toddlers than infants, such as those relating to challenging behavior or peer interactions. When you see the word *toddler* underlined within the Indicator name instead of simply "children," these are Indicators that can be scored as not applicable (N/A) for infants. In mixed-age classrooms, or even rooms with children of different developmental ages, observers should use their own judgment to determine when those Indicators are and are not appropriate for the setting and composition of the classroom.

8. CAN I CONDUCT THE OBSERVATION PORTION OF THE TPITOS OVER SEVERAL DAYS?

The TPITOS was designed to be administered in one observation session for 2 hours. By doing so, you are more likely to observe teacher practices as they typically occur. If classroom or teachers preclude you from observing for a consecutive 2 hours, you may break the observation into two sessions of at least 1 hour each. For instance, if after observing for an hour a teacher leaves the classroom and indicates she will not be returning, you may come back another time within the next day to complete that observation with another 1-hour observation period. It is not recommended that you base your scoring on any session shorter than 1 hour.

9. WHEN SHOULD I COMPLETE THE RED FLAGS?

It is recommended that you review the Red Flags before you begin your observation and consider them throughout the observation period. However, you should review and record your final Red Flag scores after completing the observation period.

10. DO I COMPLETE THE OBSERVATION OR INTERVIEW FIRST?

We recommend that the interview be conducted *after* the 2-hour observation period is complete. Many items can be scored based on observation or interview responses, and when that is the case, you must first observe. If the Indicator cannot be scored based on your observation, then you would ask the related interview question to score that Indicator.

11. CAN THE OBSERVATION AND INTERVIEW BE COMPLETED ON DIFFERENT DAYS?

The observation and interview should be conducted on the same day. The TPITOS cannot be scored completely until both the observation and the interview are completed. If unforeseen circumstances prevent you from conducting the interview on the same day as the observation, the interview may be conducted the day following the observation.

12. CAN I SET UP A VIDEO CAMERA IN THE CLASSROOM AND THEN SCORE THE OBSERVATION PORTION USING THE VIDEO?

No. To obtain valid and reliable scores, the TPITOS must be conducted *live* and in person. Scoring depends on being able to directly observe teacher practices as teachers move about and interact with all of the children in the room. A video camera in the corner of the room will likely not capture all of the practices and interactions necessary to score the TPITOS.

13. HOW CAN I FIND THE TIME TO CONDUCT THE INTERVIEW WHEN TEACHERS DO NOT HAVE TIME OUTSIDE OF THE CLASSROOM?

The interview should be conducted in person, as soon as possible after the observation, so that you and the teacher can reflect on the interactions and practices observed. If time does not allow for this, you may conduct the interview later in the day or the next day. If this is still not possible, some observers have found success conducting the interview via telephone, but this should still be completed no later than 1 day after the in-classroom observation.

14. CAN I USE THE TPITOS FOR OBSERVATIONS IN PRESCHOOL CLASSROOMS?

The TPITOS was designed to be used in infant and toddler classrooms, up to 3 years of age. We do not recommend that it be used in preschool classrooms or classrooms made up of children 3 years of age or older. There is another tool for those settings—the TPOT, which was designed to be used in classrooms serving children between 2 and 5 years of age.

15. CAN I USE THE TPITOS IN A FAMILY CHILD CARE SETTING OR OTHER MIXED-AGE SETTINGS?

The TPITOS was originally designed for use in infant–toddler classroom settings. Despite this, the TPITOS could be used with minor adaptations in family child care settings or mixed-age settings, as long as there are children from birth to 36 months of age present, and you can observe at least three of the four routines (e.g., free play, structured group, personal care practices, outdoors activities). It will be important, however, to focus your observation on those practices that teachers use specifically when interacting with infants and toddlers. If you routinely conduct the TPITOS in family child care settings, it will be important to document decisions you make about how to handle mixed-age classrooms so you can assure consistency in how the observation is administered over time and across classrooms.

16. HOW DO I KNOW WHEN TO SCORE A RED FLAG?

Red Flags are designed to be clear Indicators of poor process or structural quality. They represent practices that were either omitted or implemented in such a way that they conflict with or impede the implementation of *Pyramid Model* practices. Instances in which a Red Flag is scored should be fairly clear. Specific criteria are provided in Chapter 4 to assist in making decisions about scoring a Red Flag.

17. HOW DO I DETERMINE WHAT INFORMATION TO USE IN ORDER TO SCORE OBSERVATIONAL AND INTERVIEW ITEMS?

The manual provides explicit instructions for how to score Observational and Interview Items. These items are indicated on the Scoring Form with "Obs." and "Int." in the notes column. These are Indicators that should *first* be addressed during the observation. If observers are unable to score them based on observation, then they should ask the interview question and the response should be used in scoring that Indicator. In general, the first attempt to score the item is based on your 2-hour observation. If you are unable to score *Yes*, *No*, or *N/A* based on the observation, *only then* do you ask the related interview question after the observation is complete and score the Indicator based on the response to the interview question.

18. IF THERE ARE MULTIPLE TEACHERS IN A CLASSROOM, WHOM DO I OBSERVE?

The TPITOS was designed to be administered with only one teacher at a time. You may administer the TPITOS with all teachers in the classroom, but you would conduct one 2-hour observation and interview for each teacher individually.

19. HOW SHOULD I APPROACH SHARING TPITOS SCORES WITH TEACHERS?

The TPITOS can be used as a tool to inform coaching and professional development and as a research tool. If you are using the TPITOS as a research tool, it will be important to follow the consent procedures and research protocol used for the research study. If you are using the TPITOS for coaching or professional development purposes, we recommend that when you share TPITOS data with teachers that you communicate within the context of a collaborative relationship aimed at improving teacher and program practices. We recommend sharing information from the TPITOS as part of a coaching plan or professional focus to identify strengths and areas for improvement and to show progress over time in the implementation of *Pyramid Model* practices. TPITOS data can also be used to inform class-wide and program-wide professional development activities and assess progress in teachers' implementation of key practices over time. We recommend that coaches and teachers talk about TPITOS observations and data in the context of a collaborative coaching partnership. There should be a shared understanding about the goals or coaching and professional development, and the coach and teacher should maintain a relationship based on trust, shared focus, choice, and ongoing communication and support.

20. WHAT RESOURCES ARE AVAILABLE FOR PROVIDING COACHING AND PROFESSIONAL DEVELOPMENT TO TEACHERS ON *PYRAMID MODEL* PRACTICES?

There are two web sites that provide comprehensive training materials or information related to the *Pyramid Model*:

- National Center for Pyramid Model Innovations (NCPMI)

  http://challengingbehavior.org

  Resources include online training modules related to implementing the *Pyramid Model*, modules for training family child care providers, tip sheets, resources related to preventing suspension and expulsion, fact sheets on *Pyramid Model* research, and many other resources for families, providers, administrators, and coaches. The materials originally on the CSEFEL and TACSEI web sites are available on the NCPMI web site.

- The Pyramid Model Consortium

  http://www.pyramidmodel.org/

  The Pyramid Model Consortium provides training and technical assistance to states, communities, and programs on implementation of the *Pyramid Model* for promoting social-emotional development. Resources include online training modules related to implementing the *Pyramid Model*, modules for training family child care providers, tip sheets, resources related to preventing suspension and expulsion, fact sheets on

Pyramid Model research, and many other resources for families, providers, administrators, and coaches. Information on TPITOS Reliability Trainings can also be found on this web site.

21. HOW CAN I BECOME A CERTFIED TPITOS OBSERVER?

It is strongly recommended that individuals or groups of individuals from programs or agencies who would like to use the TPITOS in their program or as a coach become certified in use of the TPITOS. The certification process involves attending the TPITOS Reliability Training, conducted by a certified TPITOS Master Trainer who has been certified by the authors or approved as a TPITOS Trainer by the authors or publisher. Contact Brookes Publishing Company (http://www.brookespublishing.com/training/seminars/) or the Pyramid Consortium (http://www.pyramidmodel.org) to learn more about TPITOS Reliability Training and how to set up a training to meet your needs. For information on training from the publisher, please complete the Seminar Information Request Form on the publisher's web site (https://www.brookespublishing.com/seminar-information-request-form/) and/or e-mail seminars@brookespublishing.com.

Index

References to tables and figures are indicated with a *t* and *f* respectively.